A Deplorable Neanderthal Contemplates 'White Guilt'

BY RICH ROSTRON

PADOWSKI PUBLICATIONS | WOODSTOCK, IL

Contents

Introduction

The title, 'A Deplorable Neanderthal Contemplates ...' is a combination of insults cast at conservatives by the current president of the United States and a previous candidate for that position.

Sept. 9, 2016, at a campaign fundraising event, Hillary Clinton, the Democrat candidate for president against Donald Trump, referred to Trump supporters as "a basket of deplorables." The problem with her insult is that Trump supporters are not snowflakes who melt so easily. Rather than taking the insult to heart, it became a badge of honor. It was an outrageous thing to say, and probably something she had hoped would remain just between her and her supporters, but it completely backfired on her. And I've included "Deplorable" in the title because I count myself as one of those who took her insult with good humor and pride.

The same thing happened March 3, 2021, when President Biden said it was "neanderthal thinking" for Texas to open up businesses from the COVID lock down. Since that time, other states have also demonstrated that form of "neanderthal thinking," such as Florida. Rates of COVID deaths and hospitalizations have, however, proven that, if the governors of Florida and Texas have neanderthal intellects, Biden must have the intellect of Homo Erectus or some earlier species leading up to modern man.

As a conservative, I am one of those who feels that, generally, elected officials of the Democrat party have overstepped their authority and taken advantage of the Pandemic. I don't deny the existence of COVID-19, but I disagree with its handling and find many of the actions and words of so-called experts questionable.

The preceding paragraphs have made it quite clear that I'm a conservative 'Deplorable Neanderthal.' I don't deny this. In fact, I'm proud of it. But not with the inflexible thinking which the insults of Clinton and Biden would suggest. I take pride that I believe I live my life pursuing the truth. If you can convince me I'm wrong, I'll change my position. And, as the following pages demonstrate, I'm not afraid to put my ideas out there, so to speak, where others can challenge them. In fact, what is the value of one's positions if they fear allowing others to challenge them?

With this in mind, this piece is written with the idea of honestly exploring the question of 'White Guilt' that the Left has promoted in our country with increasing fervor these last 10 years or so. I have not shied away from evidence that doesn't seem to fit my position. Rather, I believe that I explore the evidence even handedly with the belief that I should let the chips fall where they may and accept the outcome as I believe we are all better off living in reality than living in a lie of my own creation.

Chapter 1
The Case of Racism Against America

"In (terms of) things racial we have always been and I believe continue to be, in too many ways, essentially a nation of cowards." [1]

—— *Former U.S. Attorney General Eric Holder*

speaking of Americans in 2009

It's funny, at 65, I can't remember a time in my life when race wasn't a prevailing issue in America. It seems to me, we have openly confronted the issues of race all my adult life. And it's quite clear that the discussion actually began long before I arrived on this earth. We haven't necessarily come up with solutions we can all agree on but, everything considered, it's difficult to see how anyone could suggest that Americans haven't fearlessly faced the issues of race and racism. But, since former Attorney General Eric Holder has posed the charge of racial cowardice, and considering the current political environment seems to suggest that others agree with him, I thought I would put down in words what, I hope, amounts to at least a modestly courageous challenge to what he, the media, and others on the Left present as a widely shared, popularly held perspective on racism today. In particular, it is my intention to challenge the notion of 'White Guilt' and Critical Race Theory (CRT) where America is seen as a "Systemically Racist" nation.

When I hear the term 'White Guilt' today, it comes

---

1 https://www.cbsnews.com/news/holder-americans-cowardly-on-race-issues/

across, to my Deplorable Neanderthal way of thinking, as a WOKEism, the popular notion that there is a correct way to view things and other perspectives are, not just wrong, but unacceptable. If one is so foolish as to continue in the face of WOKE popular culture, they are certain to face the wrath of the Cancel Culture with all the power of the digital, print and televised media. They may even find their livelihood in jeopardy. While becoming WOKE is generally a passive process that has seeped across the landscape of our society, the Cancel Culture that has grown along with it is an aggressive effort to stymie 'other' points of view. There is no caveat with the Cancel Culture that allows for opposing views that apply common sense and reason. Any – ANY – ideas that don't fit with popularly accepted concepts are verboten.

Though I disagree with Holder's contention, and find his phrasing a bit insulting, taken at face value, and giving him dramatic benefit of the doubt, I would interpret his comment as suggesting that he wants us to openly discuss racial issues with the goal of reaching consensus on how to improve racial relations moving forward. How are we to do that while the WOKE police run about canceling unwelcome perspectives? It almost suggests that Holder was giving us directions and then chuckling to himself as he steered us down a deadend street. As stated above, it seems to me we've had an extensive dialogue on race in America already. Also, as I've observed the politically connected for more than half a century, I've learned to approach such comments, such as Holder's, with a deep sense of skepticism. I'm not just asking my-self, "Does he mean what he's saying?" I'm also asking "What does he really want?"

When I saw him on the news years ago making this comment, I would have ventured a guess as to the ulterior motives behind his pronouncement. While some would suggest this shows my biases, today more than ever, I'm convinced that I see through his thinly veiled motivations.

I believe that, in 2009, Holder and his boss, President Barack Obama, were positioned at a pivotal point in history. Not since the Civil War, in terms of racial issues, has America had such a clear choice as was evident after the election of Barack Obama, especially when one path suggested a future of potentially greater racial harmony and the other, well ... greater racial disharmony? Unfortunately, it appears to me that Obama and Holder, along with their party, chose the latter. To be fair, other than Holder calling Americans racial cowards, he and Obama were saying some of the right things. Obama frequently spoke of unity and how he was elected to represent 'all Americans' regardless of their race or their party affiliation. In his 2008 acceptance speech at the Democrat National Convention, while referring to those who have historically fought to defend America, he said, "They have not served a red America or a blue America; they have served the United States of America." [2]

These, and other comments he made, were comforting

---

2 https://www.nytimes.com/2008/08/28/us/politics/28text-obama.html

words. They were words that seemed to promise a new beginning where Americans could leave the past behind and carry on together into a shiny new future where a person's race mattered less and less. But he soon said other things that seemed out of sync with that vision of unity, such as this comment from early in his first term: "They (the GOP) can come for the ride, but they gotta sit in back." [3] Or in a 2010 midterm campaign speech when he referred to 'punishing our enemies' at the polls. [4]

The thing to remember is that, and this is true when the majority of politicians speak, his comment on unity in his acceptance speech from the 2008 DNC was written by a speech writer. It was written with his campaign's ear tuned to what they thought voters wanted to hear. I call it *campaignspeak*. Did it explain how Obama truly feels? Aren't we in a better position to judge a politician's true intentions by considering their actions and what they say when their speech isn't scripted? We do have evidence that runs contrary to the warm fuzzy we received listening to him during the campaign. Some of his words and actions even seem to suggest a degree of animosity toward the nation he was elected to lead. Consider, for instance, how he sat in a pew at the Trinity United Church of Christ in Chicago where the pastor, Rev. Jeremiah Wright gave fiery sermons declaring, "Not

---

3 https://www.americanthinker.com/blog/2010/10/obama_to_gop_they_can_come_for.html
4 https://www.cbsnews.com/news/obama-explains-his-remark-about-punishing-enemies/

God Bless America but God Damn America." [5]

Obama had referred to Rev. Wright as a personal mentor but, as the 2008 Presidential campaign progressed, Obama eventually, yet mildly, disavowed himself from the 'Good Reverend' claiming that he sat in the pew for two decades but didn't really listen to what Wright was saying. Who doesn't think that's a bit of a stretch? If you've ever heard Rev. Wright and his explosive style of delivery when giving sermons, you quickly realize that a person would struggle to sleep through that if they were in a coma.

So, what does Obama really think? What was Holder's true motivation when he called Americans cowards? I believe there is one answer to both questions, and it fits a political agenda – a desire to move America further to the Left and into the realm of socialism.

As an Online article titled *Socialist Principles Have Always Been Part of Black American Tradition* puts it, "... globally speaking, the majority of socialists are not white."

A man named Z, a founder of Black Socialists of America, is quoted in the story: "I gotta say, it's not just the 'excesses' of capitalism that are disproportionately impacting us as Black Americans, but capitalism in general. As a matter of fact, capitalism always leads to these 'excesses' — they're a feature of the system!"

What does he mean by 'excesses? Z's explanation offers a literary smorgasbord of concepts: "economically speak-

---

5 https://www.newsweek.com/why-rev-wright-said-what-he-did-83979

ing, we're essentially functioning under the same relations or dynamics, albeit with different manifestations of systemic threats that can, of course, be tied to chattel slavery, Jim Crow and white supremacy ... residential segregation paired with environmental degradation and the impact these things have on the health of people in Black and Brown communities – [things like] police brutality, gentrification, food deserts, housing discrimination, etc."

While excusing what I perceive as Z's steroidal hyperbole for now, this black affinity to socialism most likely has something to do with the government providing financial assistance and enacting affirmative action presumably to benefit blacks and minorities. At the same time, these blacks see capitalism as responsible for holding them back while subjecting them to indignities and oppression. They have come to associate government involvement with positive outcomes on their behalf. If I squint just right, I can see that. The Civil Rights Act from the 1960s is a significant instance of the government asserting itself to address racism. President Lyndon Baines Johnson's 'Great Society' programs that offered financial assistance to struggling blacks would also seem to fit that narrative. There are also numerous court cases over the years that, at least eventually, were decided in favor of defending blacks from conditions seen as racist.

While considering historical grievances, it's also apparent that many black Americans struggle to this day. Considered in a vacuum, with no possibility of mitigating factors, these grievances represent powerful indictments against a nation founded on the principles of liberty. And today, it is increasingly evident that there are those among us who intend to convict the country on the charge of 'Systemic Racism' in the square of public opinion. But I find their approach extremely troubling.

When you approach the charges of America as a 'systemically racist' nation, while the 'Cancel Culture' seeks to serve as judge, jury and executioner, you are presented with an image of a kangaroo court where America is on trial while her defense attorney is muzzled and banned from the courtroom.

The 'Cancel Culture' is reinforced by a Pavlovian indoctrination from the media, the entertainment industry, education and, now, from big-tech social network giants, as well. Together, and from every direction, they hit Americans with a constant barrage of 'information' that always fits the Left's 'Narrative.' For anyone so unwise as to challenge 'the Narrative,' their very livelihoods are at risk. In some cases, the risks manifest themselves physically (For those who doubt the physical nature of the attacks, conducting Online searches of the names Andrew Duncomb and Andy Ngo will give you a taste of the evidence supporting this claim. Both are conservative journalists. Duncomb is a black American and Ngo is an Asian American).

Some on the Left have tried to dismiss the existence

of the 'Cancel Culture' as a fabrication of the Right. But others on the Left have allowed 'the secret' to slip out and have conceded that the 'Cancel Culture' is quite real. Among these are HBO's Bill Maher, Psychology Today, [6] National Review, [7] and more. I have personally experienced the Cancel Culture and, in some cases, from people who deny its existence – people who, on social networks, have attacked my business while calling me a "Racist" and "White Supremacist" for daring to challenge their WOKE mindsets.

I will not spend time debating the existence of the 'Cancel Culture' especially since I believe that doing so would bring a smile to the face of practitioners of this disturbing form of censorship – they would welcome such a diversion from the true purpose of this piece. Rather, I mention it as I see it as one of my motivations for writing this piece. The more people seek to silence others, the more inclined I am to ensure that opposing voices are heard. This is particularly true as the attacks against America's character have reached a point today that I would describe as rabid. People are attempting to shape America's future based on a one-sided perspective on racial relations and other issues. Or, more aptly put, there are those in this country who are using race, as well as those other issues, to divide Americans in order to promote a socialist agenda that would otherwise have little support.

6 https://www.psychologytoday.com/us/blog/after-service/201912/5-reasons-why-people-love-cancel-culture

7 https://www.nationalreview.com/2020/06/cancel-cancel-culture/

With this in mind, the following pages are intended as an attempt to consider America's racial past where the nation is actually allowed to present a defense, if I could so arrogantly assume to do so on America's behalf. Some may take issue that I will not expound on the charges against America in greater graphic terms. In fact, I will do little more than touch on the accusations before moving on to presenting America's defense. This is not an effort to hide from the charges. Rather, the case for the prosecution is well documented, though seldom with a fearless determination to consider all sides. There are numerous documentaries about slavery and racism in America. Stories in the news that describe apparent (but not always true) racist behavior sell and are pushed by the media. But that these stories touch our heartstrings does not prove guilt or innocence.

America was founded on principles of liberty that include the idea that someone is entitled to a fair trial, even if that individual is America herself. No doubt, there are more than a few occasions when justice was not served on behalf of black Americans though, truth be told, many white, Asian and other Americans could say the same thing. Though the nation was founded on the principle that everyone deserves a fair trial, that does not guarantee a fair trial for all. Ultimately, our legal system is still dependent on flawed individuals to administer justice and a tepid-at-best response from 'We The People' to hold them accountable. That some have abused the system over the years is a given. As

I see it, this means that liberty is not simply a right but a goal that we are responsible for defending in our lives. But if a fair trial is not guaranteed in a free society, what chance does it have when the government, and the courts, have virtually unlimited power?

Chapter 2
Guilt Just Don't Work That Way

Can you force someone to accept guilt? If you tell them that they're guilty and they need to believe it, will they? In my experience, it just doesn't work that way. It never works that way.

Guilt is a belief, an emotional response to something that has occurred in someones life where, right or wrong, they've concluded that their action, or inaction, was shameful. To reach that conclusion, to some degree, they have considered their words and/or behavior before arriving at the decision that they were wrong.

The closest you'll ever come when trying to force someone to feel guilty is to convince them to verbalize a statement of guilt. Having done so, how do you know if they mean it? How can you assess their sincerity? You can lead a horse to water, but you can't make it drink. Using this metaphor, while the horse probably knows that is water you've led it to, it's another thing to convince someone that their guilt is flowing over the riverbed.

While you can't force someone to accept guilt, if they're willing, you may convince them to consider the possibility of guilt. To do so, you need to persuade them to honestly consider the evidence. You may help lay out the evidence with the hope that they'll arrive at 'the appropriate conclusion.' This is a scenario that often applies to children. Parents want their children to learn from their mistakes and they'll say things, such as, "Now don't you feel guilty?"

Children are more apt than many to provide the desired answer but then it's still a question, not only whether they're just saying what their parents want to hear, but also whether they really understand? Does a parent accept their admission of guilt as enough? This is why many parents are skeptical of such admissions of guilt. It also helps to explain why punishments are not always defrayed by a child admitting his or her guilt.

As for adults, we're most apt to see such instances when someone is convicted of a crime. Prior to passing sentence, a judge may try to determine if the guilty party feels remorse (guilt) over what they have done. But the judge seldom has anything to go on other than the words and demeanor of the convicted? A criminal who is a good actor can often play this situation to their advantage as, no doubt, has been done on numerous occasions. As with a child, however, the sincerity with which someone feels repentant requires an honest appraisal of the situation at hand.

Additionally, we cannot assume that, when someone tries to make someone else accept guilt about something, that the effort is sincere. Just as it is possible for someone to pose as guilt-ridden, it also occurs that someone will try to fill someone with guilt where little or none is justified. The question this begs to answer is, "Why?" Why would someone want to convince someone to accept and embrace guilt? Even when the guilt is justified, why would one person seek to convince another to accept guilt?

The answer is obvious: they have an ulterior motive and are seeking to achieve some goal that is only possible when someone else feels guilty. They want the person who accepts the guilt to do something, or to stand by and do nothing, for some specific reason. Even if the only action they want is the knowledge that the other person accepts responsibility, the only reason to try to convince someone of guilt is in order to achieve something specific. For instance, the family of a murder victim may want to know that the killer is remorseful. But the motivations to convince someone of guilt are not always as understandable or acceptable. In some cases, such as I believe we are experiencing in America today, there are those using guilt as a weapon against other Americans in order to convince them to surrender to ideas without full and complete examination.

Chapter 3
GET YOUR WHITE GUILT HERE!

In America today, there are those in our society pushing 'White Guilt.' As I understand it, the notion is that this guilt is based on 'White Privilege.' They want white Americans to feel guilty and, as stated above, they have a specific reason for wanting this. There's little disagreement that the leading proponents of this push are those on the Left. I believe they are using race to divide Americans in order to transform America into a socialist nation (the strategy is called "Divide and Conquer"). For instance, the three Founders of Black Lives Matter, Patrisse Kahn-Cullors, Alicia Garza and Opal Tometi, have openly stated that they are trained Marxist and that their goal is to transform America into a Marxist nation (at least one of the three, Kahn-Cullors, muddied up the message a bit by using large sums of the donations to the group to purchase multiple, lavish estates, one alone valued at \$1.4 million [8]).

Putting the politics aside for just a moment, the premise is that America should have dealt with its 'White Privilege' long ago and thereby have avoided her 'White Guilt.' Her guilt is based on this 'failure,' which manifested itself as slavery, Jim Crow, Segregation, lynching, verbal and physical assaults, etc. The degree to which the Left wants the government to respond to America's

8 https://nypost.com/2021/04/10/inside-blm-co-founder-patrisse-khan-cullors-real-estate-buying-binge/

guilt assumes that the government will have the power to rectify the matter. This assumption requires the government to have more power than many believe we can safely assume to trust the government with. Those pushing 'White Guilt' have made it clear that it is racist to suggest the government should lack the power and authority to respond to the situation and if the government needs additional power to do so, then such power must be given. It is based on these notions that the battle lines are drawn, the one side seeking to restrain the power of the government (and labeled 'racists' for their efforts) while the other side uses race to shake more power loose from the people and into the hands of the government where it can, presumably, serve 'the greater good.'

If we accept the WOKE notions of 'White Guilt' and CRT, all white Americans have benefited from their whiteness – their 'White Privilege' – and they all have 'White Guilt.' In reaction to this guilt, a few years ago, we were seeing news stories about whites who were stopping blacks on the streets so the whites could get down on their knees and clean the blacks' shoes, or was it their feet (possibly symbolizing Jesus washing the feet of his disciples).

With all this talk about 'White Privilege,' CRT and 'White Guilt' we know there must be something to it, right? But especially since there are those pushing white Americans to accept and embrace this guilt, doesn't it make sense for us to question whether the guilt is justified, even though we're told not to pose such 'inflammatory' questions? If nothing else, if whites are to feel sincere remorse, can they do so just because they're told that they should? The only way to mean it when whites express their guilt is to consider what they're guilty of, and why, so that they understand what they've done and what they should do now to set things right.

This, therefore, is one of the goals I seek over the course of the following pages. On a personal level, it is my desire to honestly consider the question though I admit to certain inclinations from the start. Those inclinations are in the form of skepticisms based on certain prejudices. But I see those prejudices not as racial bigotry but rather as political positions by which I disagree with and do not trust the Left, as you may have already gathered. In spite of these predispositions, I intend to honestly consider the question so that I can arrive at a conclusion that I can espouse without losing the ability to look myself in the mirror without flinching. My hope is that the following pages will help you to do the same, even if you don't come to the same conclusions when you've finished reading.

Chapter 4
Is 'White Guilt' Real?

The only way to determine if 'White Guilt' is real is to consider the question honestly. This does not fit the Left's approach where 'Cancel Culture' insists that whites accept their guilt without asking too many questions. The first question I have, therefore, is why does the Left want whites to unquestioningly accept guilt?

As mentioned previously, without an honest appraisal, it is extremely unlikely that someone will reach a point of sincere remorse. The only way to ensure a sincere sense of guilt, if that is appropriate, is to demand a thorough investigation of the charges. But when someone shies away from 'looking too closely,' their attitude suggests fear; they are afraid that an honest appraisal will not bring people around to their desired conclusion. They lack the confidence to lay out the evidence and allow people to arrive at their own conclusions.

With confidence that the evidence will assuredly bring white people around to accept their guilt, the Left would reverse their 'Cancel Culture' and do everything possible to ensure everyone has a full and unfettered access to the evidence. This is not the same as watching documentaries on PBS about the black experience in America. It's not just about the material created by academia on the subjects of slavery, Jim Crow and social ills in our society. This is a question of making the connection between what has occurred, the appropriate degree of guilt and determining who the guilty parties are.

Keep in mind that, when someone wants you to accept guilt, they always have a specific motive behind that desire. Whether that motive is noble, or even reasonable, is a subjective question, as is the idea that white Americans need to accept 'White Guilt.' What are the motivations of those seeking to convince others to feel guilty? In the case of 'White Guilt,' how will the acceptance of this guilt by whites improve racial relations in America? Or will it? Is it even intended to do so? Keep these questions in mind as you continue along with this Deplorable Neanderthal in the contemplation of 'White Guilt.'

Chapter 5
Case for the Prosecution

As mentioned earlier, I don't believe we need to spend a lot of time arguing over whether many blacks have experienced injustice and harsh treatment in America. There is no denying that America's hands are not entirely clean in terms of racial relations over the course of her 239-year history (as of this writing, 1783-2022). The list of transgressions is long and includes ...

• Slavery (predating the War for Independence and the signing of the constitution)
• The 3/5ths Compromise that reinforced the institution of slavery in the constitution
• Eighty years of slavery from the signing of the constitution to the Emancipation Proclamation
• The brutal treatment of slaves and blacks before and after the Civil War
• The lynching of free blacks following the Civil War
• Jim Crow and Segregation that, arguably, lasted until LBJ signed the Civil Rights Act of 1964 (you could say for 100 years)
• Continued racial discrimination in the years afterwards

This is quite a litany of offenses. Television documentaries and educational material have gone a long way to bringing these charges to life – demonstrating the very real nature of this abhorrent treatment. There is no denying that there is not a basis in fact for these accusations. How then would anyone be so bold as to persist in offering a defense?

We can imagine a prosecuting attorney reading these charges to a stunned courtroom. The defendant, America, and their defense attorney would obviously feel that they faced an uphill battle defending themselves from such charges. That's especially true since, as mentioned above, few who would argue that the charges aren't, to varying degrees, true. But, referring back to our parental analogy, a good parent would still want to hear the defendant out. In other words, America still has a right to present a defense.

America has a right to expect those condemning her to consider all the facts – the good, the bad and any factors that might shine a mitigating light on America's involvement in these crimes.

Having presented the charges, abiding by the current Cancel Culture, the prosecution has essentially chosen to rest. The essence of the Cancel Culture is to suggest that there is no possible defense and, therefore, no need to waste our time on such trivialities. If a defense was justified, the Left would have acknowledged as much while levying the charges. But, as was pointed out earlier, some of us simply refuse to quietly accept that premise; we insist on an opportunity to present a defense and it is now the defense's turn to present arguments that establish where guilt is and/or isn't appropriately applied, and the degree to which it is justified.

Chapter 6
Opening Arguments for the Defense

What possible defense could America present? Trying to tackle all the charges at once offers an approach that is both cumbersome and difficult to follow. Attempting to do so would, no doubt, appease the proponents of the Cancel Culture. But though this is a relatively short work, America still deserves a more thoughtful appraisal of the charges – an honest appraisal where the charges are addressed one at a time.

Recently a writer, who is widely celebrated by the Left, has suggested that slavery in the 'New Continent' began in 1619 (the argument posed by CRT) and that this introduction of slavery into America defines the nation ever since, even though the United States of America didn't actually come into existence until more than a century-and-a-half later (additionally, even by the author's description, the initial slaves were not slaves at all but "indentured servants" from Africa who later achieved freedom). No doubt, America's 'White Guilt' begins with whites arriving from across the seas and introducing slavery into this peaceful paradise where native Americans had existed in harmony for several epochs. That makes sense. We all know that, along with smallpox, Europeans brought slavery to the shores of this continent. Or do we know that?

In a Feb. 2, 2020, article in History Today titled 'Slaves and Indians: Europeans did not introduce slavery to

North America – although they did change the way it was practiced,' [9] writer Edward Mair refers to Frederick Douglass's 'My Bondage and My Freedom' written in 1855. Douglass acknowledged that the institution of slavery existed on the continent prior to the arrival of the white man while arguing that, among the Native Americans, it was "more lenient." Mair explains that "Native American slaveholding was in fact an institution with a long history that was rarely as compassionate as Douglass thought."

Suffice it to say that, before whites arrived, Native Americans took slaves, often in battle between tribes. This, of course, doesn't absolve Americans of all guilt for having slavery but it does bring a mitigating factor into the discussion, especially where America's guilt over slavery often seems to exist in a historical vacuum.

According to a March 6, 2018, Smithsonian Magazine article, [10] black slaves owned by Cherokees were among those who suffered on the Trail of Tears. The article even names one such Native American slaveowner – Chief John Ross.

The article also refers to "Choctaw Chief Greenwood LeFlore (who) had 15,000 acres of Mississippi land ... and 400 enslaved African Americans under his dominion." The story goes on to explain that "all five of the 'so-called Civilized Tribes' (Cherokee, Chickasaw, Choctaw, Creek and Seminole)" had black slaves.

9 https://www.historytoday.com/archive/feature/slaves-and-indians
10 https://www.smithsonianmag.com/smithsonian-institution/how-native-american-slaveholders-complicate-trail-tears-narrative-180968339/

These tribes "were deeply committed to slavery, established their own racialized black codes, immediately re-established slavery when they arrived in Indian territory, rebuilt their nations with slave labor, crushed slave rebellions, and enthusiastically sided with the Confederacy in the Civil War."

African-American Historian Tiya Miles is quoted in the story as suggesting that the Native Americans owned black slaves as a way to show their societal sophistication to white settlers. That, however, seems a rather flimsy justification when one considers the way the politically correct Cancel Culture today demonstrates absolute intolerance and lack of forgiveness for white Americans. How can Americans, 156 years after the Civil War, find no refuge from the guilt of slavery while Native Americans who actually owned slaves are absolved of guilt with such a weak excuse? And slavery was not just confined to the American continent.

In an Online search of 'Slavery in Africa,' the top search result is from Wikipedia. The snippet under the search result reads, "Slavery has historically been widespread in Africa. Systems of servitude and slavery were common in parts of Africa in ancient times." And, as is widely documented, blacks brought to America as slaves were sold to the slave traders by blacks who captured them in Africa.

In an undated article in CornellResearch, writer Jackie Swift reviews Sandra Greene's writing on the history of slavery in West Africa, titled 'The Curious History of

Slavery in Africa.' Swift writes that "Very few Americans know that slavery was common throughout the world as well as in Africa." [11]

Greene writes, "Slavery in the United States ended in 1865 but in West Africa it was not legally ended until 1875, and then stretched unofficially until almost WWI."

Greene goes on to write, "While 11 to 12 million people are estimated to have been exported as slaves from West Africa (very many going to places in the world other than the Americas) ... millions more were retained (as slaves) in Africa."

Of course, most of us are familiar with slavery in Ancient Egypt and how slaves were used to build the pyramids. Another undated article in Restavek Freedom titled, 'History of Slavery Part 1 – Slavery in Ancient Times,' explains that "Slavery in ancient times typically came about as a result of debt, birth into a slave family, child abandonment, war or as a punishment for a crime."

The article goes on to explain that, "Sumer or Sumeria is still thought to be the birthplace of slavery." Slavery was common in Mesopotamia. As Part 2 of the article states, slavery was common in the Middle Ages in Europe and Asia. [12]

During the reign of King Charlemagne, "European slaves became wildly popular throughout Muslim countries, marking the true beginning of the global slave trade." In Asia, pirates and soldiers of the Tang Dynasty

11 https://research.cornell.edu/news-features/curious-history-slavery-west-africa
12 https://restavekfreedom.org/2018/08/02/history-of-slavery-part-2-slavery-in-the-middle-ages/

"also took countless slaves in raids of Korea, Turkey, Persia and Indonesia as well as thousands of slaves taken from indigenous Aboriginal tribes."

At the very least, this little history lesson confirms that America did not invent slavery. Historically, she came in on the tail end of the institution, to the degree that it has ended in the world (it's important to note that it has not completely ended). In fact, an honest appraisal of the institution of slavery shows that the entire human race bears a share of guilt over the issue of slavery. Or does it?

Throughout history, the world was not divided between slaves and slave holders. It's probably safe to assume that the majority of people throughout history were neither slaves nor slaveholders. The same is certainly true of America.

Of course, with the 3/5ths Compromise, America did make slavery legal in the Southern States or, more aptly put, allowed slavery to continue in the Southern States.

Chapter 7
The 3/5ths Compromise
and American Slavery

Before the ink had dried on the constitution, the anti-slavery movement was agitating to end the institution in the new nation (in reality, the fight against slavery began well before that). Clearly, many of the signers of the constitution saw slavery as a repugnant institution and regretted they were unable to end the practice with the creation of a new form of government.

In the Wikipedia article, 'Founding Fathers of the United States,' [13] it is explained that many of the Founders were opposed to slavery and "predicted that the issue would threaten to tear the country apart."

A Sept. 6, 2020, article in 'The Source' titled 'What does the constitution say about slavery and the shocking number of Founding Fathers who tried to dead (sic) slave trade in the 18th Century,' [14] the claim is made that "In fact, some of the founding fathers (36 out of the 39 framers) actually were opposed to slavery." Whether that number is accurate or not, it is clear that there were Founding Fathers who were not in favor of slavery.

The Wikipedia 'Founding Fathers ...' article explains that George Washington, while an owner of slaves, "gradually became a cautious supporter of abolitionism and freed his slaves in his will."

13 https://en.wikipedia.org/wiki/Founding_Fathers_of_the_United_States
14 https://thesource.com/2020/09/06/constitution-slavery-founding-fathers/

The same article goes on to explain that "John Jay led the successful fight to outlaw the slave trade in New York."

Other Founding Fathers who actively opposed the institution of slavery included, but are not limited to:

- Samuel Adams
- John Adams
- Benjamin Rush
- Stephen Hopkins (who introduced the earliest anti-slavery laws in the Colonies)
- Alexander Hamilton
- Thomas Paine
- And numerous others

Even President Thomas Jefferson, frequently called out as a slave owner by the Left today, "called for and signed into law a Federally-enforced ban on the international slave trade throughout the U.S. and its territories."

The 1619 Project has claimed that the American Revolution was actually fought to protect the institution of slavery in America from Parliament of King George III's effort to end slavery in America. But that doesn't fit with the written record either. Consider the efforts of colonies to end slavery even before the Revolution began. Examples of this are found in Richard M. Ketchum's book, 'The Winter Soldiers: The Battles for Trenton and Princeton.' He writes, "The Massachusetts assembly in 1774 had voted to abolish the slave trade (a decision negated by veto of the royal governor); Rhode Island, declaring that 'those who are desirous of enjoying all the advantages of liberty themselves should be willing to extend personal liberty to others,' ruled that any slaves imported into the colony would be freed; Connecticut did likewise; Delaware prohibited importation; and Pennsylvania taxed the slave trade out of existence."

Once again, the fact that some were against slavery doesn't necessarily absolve America of guilt. Or does it?

Who created and maintained the anti-slavery movement for all those years extending back into Colonial days? These organizations long pre-dated the Civil War and even the activism of Frederick Douglass. Had white men not maintained these groups, where would Douglass have found a platform to take a stand against slavery while demonstrating his incredible oratory skills and intellect.

Chapter 8
From Constitution
to Emancipation

The reality is that slavery was a contradiction to the constitutional notion of liberty. As many Founders predicted, it eventually led to a war that tore the nation apart. But the war wouldn't have happened if many Americans weren't willing to honestly consider the issue. It festered as a sore on America's collective conscience because America had a conscience.

To uniformly convict Americans of the guilt of slavery is to ignore that, if not for Americans and the notion of liberty, what would have motivated anyone to contest the issue so vociferously? How would slavery have ever ended in this country?

What price did America pay for slavery? The immediate apparent cost was the Civil War. Many of us are familiar with the number 620,000 as representing the number of Americans who died in that bloody war. The overwhelming majority of those who died were white men, members of the group that receives the most blame in our current 'White Guilt' culture. But, before we move on, let us examine that number a little closer.

Under closer inspection, we discover that 620,000 dead Americans represented:

• 1 out of every 50 Americans alive at the time
• 1 out of every 4.4 Americans who fought in the war
• An approximately equal number who were seriously wounded and often incapacitated by their wounds from the war
• 6.2-million dead Americans if the same war were fought today, and Americans died at the same rate

The additional costs to America also come in terms of her conscience. In this regard, as the end of slavery did not see, what we would call, the rapid normalization of racial relations, it has included an on-going sense of guilt due to the way many blacks were treated (once again, without that American conscience, talk of racial equality would fall on deaf ears even today). The wound has festered. As a result, and in your Deplorable Neanderthal author's opinion, there are those who have long sought to take advantage of the emotions of fair-minded Americans.

What this proves is that America is not that kid who steadfastly refuses to consider their behavior. For as much as America has committed wrongs, she has also consistently and courageously considered her behavior and fought against those urges and behaviors that are not consistent with her principles of liberty. Americans overwhelmingly strive for fairness. A nation that spends its entire history wrestling with the issue of race is NOT 'inherently racist.'

Consider that the Congress that voted to free the slaves,

and extended to black men the right to vote (as well as women in 1912) was comprised almost exclusively of white men. White men, though they receive little or no credit for it, were also the standard bearers in the fight against Jim Crow and Segregation.

That white men, along with black men, and women of both colors, had to carry on the fight against those post-war racist institutions was due to the attitudes and behavior, primarily, of a particular group of white men. But can that blanket all white men, or America, with the same brush of guilt? Should we convict the white men who fought against slavery along with the slave owners?

America deserves credit for never abandoning the fight for better racial relations. I believe that the benefits of this tenacity extend beyond our own borders. Yes, Britain ended slavery in most of its colonies in 1833 (the Slavery Abolition Act) but there are questions about her motives at the time. France ended slavery in 1794 but Napoleon Bonaparte rolled back that decision in 1802. It wasn't until 1848 that France banned slavery but only in its colonies.

The immutable fact is that America set the standard for the concept of individual liberty in practice rather than merely in theory. It was after America won its independence that the concept of liberty began to spread beyond our shores. The shot fired on Lexington Green in April of 1775 is called "The Shot Heard Round the World" for a reason. It initiated a war for liberty and that liberty, while introducing the idea of the rights of the individual, made the contradiction of slavery real everywhere for anyone willing to honestly consider the issue. As the concept of liberty spread and, as long as slavery existed, it was impossible to entirely hide from that contradiction.

The 3/5ths Compromise was where the Founders had run headlong into that contradiction. It appears they dodged the question, though it is easier for us to say so from our relative safety looking back into the past. In any case, the 3/5ths Compromise was a bandage on a sore that was left to fester.

So why did the Founders accept this morally deficient and problematic compromise? Clearly, their focus was on unity. During the War for Independence, one of the battle cries of the Colonists was "We will stand together or we will surely fall apart!" The war was won, but the Founders were wise enough to realize that America was a fledgling entrant among the community of nations; their security was not guaranteed. After fighting for more than eight years, no one wanted to sacrifice their independence, or the blood shed to gain that liberty, in the face of global challengers.

As we mentioned previously, many of the Founders were opposed to slavery. Some assumed that the institution of slavery would simply fade away economically. If not for Eli Whitney and the patent of his cotton gin in 1794, it's possible they would have been correct. Instead, his invention is credited with changing the financial landscape related to slavery; it made slavery more economically viable in the South where cotton was a prominent crop and part of the economy.

There was also a sense among the Founders that mounting opposition to slavery would eventually put sufficient pressure on slaveholders and slave states to the extent that they would abandon the practice. Failing that, many of the Founders astutely prophesized that the contradiction would eventually tear the country apart.

The Other Servitude

The correct term for 'the other servitude' in colonial and early America is 'indentured servant.' As mentioned earlier, the original black slaves brought to this country in 1619 were actually indentured servants who eventually won their freedom. But indentured servants were largely white. Certainly, indentured servitude had an advantage over those living in a state of slavery – indentured servants were bound to their 'masters' for a specific period of time. There was an assumption of freedom at the termination of that specific period. There was no such assumption of freedom for slaves. Theirs was a life of slavery where the only salvation from slavery was death or physical incapacitation. But there were significant similarities between indentured servants and slaves.

Indentured servants could not pick up and leave without their master's permission. Doing so made an outlaw of the indentured servant who was so bold or rash. If caught trying to run away, it was likely to extend the period of servitude. It was also likely to bring on significant punishments, as well. And, even without running away, indentured servants could experience harsh treatment at the hands of their 'masters.'

Chapter 9
Slavery and the Whip

The whip was the instrument of choice used to administer the most historically familiar form of punishment from the days of slavery. The whip had the advantage of serving to painfully reinforce authority without causing lasting physical harm. Slaveholders did not want to damage 'their property' beyond 'its usefulness' but to control it. The whip, however, was not reserved solely for slaves or on a racial basis.

Floggings were common punishments for infractions committed by sailors and soldiers in armies and navies around the world. As explained in the Naval History and Heritage Command Website's article titled 'Brief History of Punishment by Flogging in the US Navy,' "A proposal to abolish flogging (in the U.S. Navy) was first introduced in Congress in 1820 by Representative Samuel Foot, but it was unsuccessful." [15]

In 1845, John Hale of New Hampshire was elected to the U.S. Senate. An opponent of slavery, Hale introduced a bill to end floggings in the Navy. Spurred by Hale's actions, and activities of other opponents of floggings, in 1850, the Secretary of the Navy, "… sent an inquiry to a number of naval officers asking for their opinions on whether flogging and grog could be eliminated without damage to the Navy."

---

15 https://www.history.navy.mil/research/library/online-reading-room/title-list-alphabetically/b/brief-history-punishment-flogging-us-navy.html

That same year, Herman Melville, the famed author of Moby Dick, wrote a book called 'White Jacket' that included a chapter that described the effects of floggings. In 1855, Congress passed a law revising forms of discipline in the Navy that specifically did not include flogging. In 1862, the new rules were made official.

Still, use of the whip appears to have been common against black slaves in the Antebellum South. And use of the whip continued, to some degree, following the war.

Chapter 10
Lynching and
Post Civil War Oppression

The oppression of many blacks at the hands of their former 'masters' continued after the war. A key form of oppression came with the lynching of freed blacks. Once again, however, as with the whip, the rope was not reserved exclusively for black necks.

According to the NAACP – Archives at Tuskegee Institute, between 1882 and 1968, 4,743 individuals were lynched in the United States. Approximately three out of every four instances involved the lynching of a black (1,297 whites and 3,446 blacks). [16] There were states, however, where the majority of those lynched were whites:

States Where More Whites Were Lynched Than Blacks

State	Whites	Blacks
Arizona	31	0
California	41	2
Colorado	65	3
Idaho	20	0
Indiana	33	14
Iowa	17	2
Kansas	35	19
Maine	1	0
Michigan	7	1
Minnesota	5	4
Montana	82	2
Nebraska	52	5
Nevada	6	0
New Mexico	33	3
North Dakota	13	3
Oklahoma	82	40
Oregon	20	1
South Dakota	27	0
Utah	6	2
Vermont	1	0
Washington	25	1
Wisconsin	6	0
Wyoming	30	5
Total	638	107

---

16 http://law2.umkc.edu/faculty/projects/ftrials/shipp/lynchingsstate.html

In these 23 of the 40 states where the statistics applied, 638 whites were hung in comparison to 107 blacks. But there were six other states where the numbers did not necessarily demonstrate a racial component in regard to the individuals who were lynched:

States With Nominal Difference in Race of those Lynched		
State	Whites	Blacks
Delaware	0	1
Illinois	15	19
New Jersey	1	1
New York	1	1
Ohio	10	16
Pennsylvania	2	6
Total	29	44

In those 6 states, the difference, as shown above, was 29 whites to 44 blacks.

Where the numbers are skewed sharply in the other direction is in the Southern States, the states that fought on the side of the Confederacy. In the states that did not side with the Confederacy, there were 667 whites who were lynched and 151 blacks. In the former Confederate states, 630 whites were lynched compared to 3,295 blacks.

This is a period of time when capital punishment was common for crimes, such as murder. The sentence was frequently carried out at the end of a rope. Setting aside the reader's personal perspective on capital punishment, this does not absolve anyone of guilt for a lynching that was not in response to a legitimate capital offense or where race entered into the decision to hang someone. But, for those who think of lynching as solely reserved for use against blacks, these figures may add a touch of a perspective.

The reality is that the overwhelming majority of Americans during the time were not involved in a lynching of any kind, 'legal' or otherwise, black or white. While most of these people were busy living their own lives, and had other priorities, those who were involved likely took part in more than one lynching. To what degree are we to hold the masses of the prior accountable for the actions of the infinitesimally small latter group?

There is no doubt that lynching was a tool used in some states to intimidate and control blacks. Some have reasonably speculated that the death of Abraham Lincoln spelled doom for Reconstruction in the Southern States. If true, this may help to explain why the South devolved into Jim Crow and Segregation.

Chapter 11
100 years of Jim Crow and Segregation

Jim Crow laws are traced back to the contested election of Rutherford B. Hayes as president of the United States (1876). A tie in the Electoral College was decided when a deal was struck where Hayes, a Republican and staunch abolitionist, was named president over opponent and Democrat Samuel J. Tilden. As part of the agreement, Federal troops enforcing reconstruction were removed from the Southern States.

With the removal of the Federal troops, the teeth were pulled from the Civil Rights Act of 1875. That law had prohibited discrimination in theaters, public transportation and other public places (in 1883, the Supreme Court ruled that the Civil Rights Act of 1875 was unconstitutional, that the constitution prohibited states but not individuals from discriminating).

In 1896, the Court ruled in the Plessy v Ferguson case. The ruling came to be known as the 'Separate But Equal Clause.' In 1909, the NAACP was founded at a conference in New York City. Beginning in 1913, President Woodrow Wilson began segregation of the U.S. military. According to the NAACP, in 1925, there were 3 million members of the KKK, though it's difficult to know how they arrived at that number considering the secrecy of the organization. At the time, the population of the U.S. was 114.2 million. [17] Therefore, even if the NAACP's figures

17 https://mste.illinois.edu/malcz/ExpFit/data.html

were somehow accurate, only 2.6 percent of Americans belonged to the KKK. Or put another way, if 3 million Americans were members of the organization, 111.2 million were not. How then do we condemn the total based on the behavior of a sliver of a minority, even though the actions of the former, the KKK members, were so despicable? Even if we assume there was an additional group that sympathized with the KKK, there was still a larger group that did not.

Chapter 12
Charles Hamilton Houston

Charles Hamilton Houston (1895-1950) was a black lawyer known as 'The man who killed Jim Crow." He is also known for mentoring future Supreme Court Justice Thurgood Marshall. Houston was involved in nearly every case involving Jim Crow and Civil Rights from 1930 until his death. He argued against Plessy v Ferguson's "Separate But Equal" clause as particularly unfair in regards to education. Though he had passed by then, his arguments were instrumental in the decision Brown v Board of Education Topeka (1954) where the Supreme Court ruled school segregation was unconstitutional.

Houston is one example of how there were blacks who fought strenuously against Jim Crow. But, as a 2019 Washington Post article explains, "White activists were largely overlooked but strategically essential" in the fight against Jim Crow. [18] This article specifically refers to the 1963 March on Washington, D.C., when Martin Luther King Jr. made his "I have a dream" speech, but the point is clearly indicative of the movement as a whole.

In June 2007, Jenni Burch, of Grove City, OH, wrote to the Ferris State University Jim Crow Museum. She pointed out that the museum seemed to exclusively portray whites as bad and blacks as good. Curator David

---

18 https://www.washingtonpost.com/lifestyle/style/in-march-on-washington-white-activists-were-largely-overlooked-but-strategically-essential/2013/08/25/f2738c2a-eb27-11e2-8023-b7f07811d98e_story.html

Pilgrim replied writing of Jonathan Myrick Daniels who played a significant role in the fight against Jim Crow. Daniels was a white man and VMI grad who underwent a spiritual conversion while at church one day in 1962. He became a minister and "was drawn to the 'Social Gospel' - ... a socio-theological movement" applying Christian principles to social problems, such as poverty, inequality, racism and war. Daniels was killed pushing a young black teenager to the floor when a store owner opened fire with a shotgun. The teen, and another, had tried to order sodas at a 'White-Only' counter. The shooter was found not guilty by an all-white jury.

Early in his response, Pilgrim writes, "The 'morality play' involved many Americans and there were whites on both sides." [19]

Some might find that a carefully nuanced response. The reality is that, without massive support of whites, both active and passive, throughout the fight against Jim Crow and Segregation, there was no way that those race-based aspects of American society would have ended. Additionally, Pilgrim seems to suggest that the only way a white person in America could be 'good' is if they were deeply active in the Civil Rights movement. Does it make someone bad, or do they fall short of 'good', if they have other priorities? By today's standards, that would appear to be the case. In years gone by, however, when people felt they had a right to choose the course of their own lives, this wasn't a widely shared perspective (it's

---

19 https://www.ferris.edu/HTMLS/news/jimcrow/question/2007/june.htmP

not one that I share now – I don't believe anyone else has the right to determine the priorities in my life).

The 1960 U.S. Census found that 88.6 percent of the total population at the time was non-Hispanic white. The immutable fact is that white support was a prerquisite for any legislative actions in the U.S. That includes measures taken in regard to race.

In the 86th U.S. Congress of 1960, there were three black Democrats in Congress. Obviously, they did not have the power, on their own, to pass laws that would end Jim Crow and Segregation; they required the support of a near majority of whites in the House and a majority in the Senate. In 1964, when the Civil Rights Act was passed, there were four black Democrats in the House. The Act passed the House by a vote of 290-130 (Feb. 10, 1964) and the Senate by a vote of 73-27 (June 19, 1964).

Here is the breakdown of the vote by party in both houses ... [20]

1964 Civil Rights Act

How they voted ...

Senate	Democrat	Republican
Yeah	46	27
Nay	21	6

House	Democrat	Republican
Yeah	152	138
Nay	96	34

20 https://www.wsj.com/articles/ SB1041302509432817073?fbclid=IwAR2pyWLMRo1QReh-O0vdlcCpLAsOZcSiiugeerghB2H5jxKlZnK63EGljso

Broken down based on racial demographics, four blacks voted in favor of the Civil Rights Act while 259 whites voted for the bill. While blacks had a limited presence in the federal government, whites carried the day in defense of the rights of blacks and minorities in America. Proportionally, Republicans showed the strongest support for the measure.

Chapter 13
Racial Relations after Jim Crow

Once again, it would be wonderful to say that, with the passing of the Civil Rights Act, Americans came together in a color-blind 'Kumbaya' moment and lived happily ever after. That is not how it worked out. Nor, do I believe, was that a reasonable expectation.

Redlining that kept blacks from buying homes in certain neighborhoods continued. Busing of black children into predominantly white schools was a hotly contested issue for about a decade. In the '90s, an anti-crime bill was passed that many on the Left, while ignoring their role in the passage of that law, now portray as racially motivated. At the same time, and related to that law, blacks today argue they are unfairly targeted by the police. There are also complaints that exceptional black students are not recognized and equally advanced with exceptional white students.

In 1994, President Bill Clinton (D) signed the Violent Crime Control and Law Enforcement Act into law. [21] In the 2020 presidential campaign, former VP and current President Joe Biden found himself trying to explain away why he authored that law, which is blamed for mass incarceration of blacks in the years following the passage of the law (his success can only be attributed to a press

21 https://www.aclu.org/blog/smart-justice/mass-incarceration/
how-1994-crime-bill-fed-mass-incarceration-crisis?fbclid=IwAR0ZSvnrm-
kQkykx26AhTcfQ8F8DzApt8bPmYXktyDXxgL5I3CW9Kohe1jig

that operated on his behalf as a Democrat rather than providing unbiased coverage during the presidential campaign). The House that passed the Act consisted of 258 Democrats, 176 Republicans and 1 Independent. The Senate was also controlled by Democrats (57 Democrats to 43 Republicans). In the Senate, two Republicans and two Democrats voted against the bill (one Dem did not vote). In the House, the vote was much closer and far more partisan. The House passed the bill by a vote of 235-195. Of the 235 votes in favor of the bill, 188 were cast by Democrats, 46 by Republicans and one by an Independent. Of the 195 who voted against the bill, 64 were Democrats and 131 were Republicans (four Democrats and one Republican didn't vote in the House). [22]

Black activists now point to the Violent Crime Control and Law Enforcement Act as an example of 'systemic racism' in America. But the breakdown of the vote shows that Democrats, who claim to be the champions of minorities in America, were the chief supporters of the bill. In fact, the bill is alternately known as the 'Biden Crime Bill' or the 'Clinton Crime Law.' Either the bill was not racially motivated, or the Democrats were hiding their racism while passing it into law.

In reality, it was perceived of as a law that would benefit minorities who lived in the most violent neighborhoods. An April 8, 2016, Online article by NBC writer Yolanda Young, argued that, "But if Bill and Hillary Clinton were the pot (for their support, and Bill's signing of the law),

____

22 https://www.govtrack.us/congress/votes/103-1994/h416

black politicians, activists, and pastors were the kettle. Their support of punitive measures actually paved the way for Clinton." [23] Even the media was behind the law at the time of its passage.

The media was running story after story about violent crime in inner-city neighborhoods. Americans were clamoring for something to be done about the situation. Considering that the majority of violent crimes were committed by and against blacks, white support for the bill can be seen as intended to benefit blacks and African American communities. But apparently, it hasn't worked out that way.

Doesn't it really come down to a question of the law's application; does racism play a role in how the law is applied?

Activists for racial equality have made claims of significant racial disparity in the application of the law. But the data doesn't clearly support that contention. Additionally, the data suggests the situation is improving dramatically.

As of Saturday, Feb. 20, 2021, the racial breakdown of inmates in federal prisons included 57.6 percent whites and 38.6 percent blacks (2.4 percent Native American and 1.5 percent Asian). [24] Of course, those numbers, when compared to national-racial demographics, show a higher incarceration rate for blacks. But that doesn't

23 https://www.nbcnews.com/news/nbcblk/analysis-black-leaders-supported-clinton-s-crime-bill-n552961

24 https://www.bop.gov/about/statistics/statistics_inmate_race.jsp?fbclid=I-wAR3rH5L0VD5oLZP1gsgruKirh0FmbO3UTMb7g43oamlZ_RNPsyHGjg-v92A

take into account crime rates by race. But, when considering the data from a Dec. 4, 2019, Washington Post article, the improvement cannot be overstated. That story, which considered incarceration in state prisons from 2000 to 2019, shows that the disparity of black vs. white incarceration fell from 8.3-times higher for blacks than whites to 5.1-to-1. [25]

The story goes on to show that blacks were imprisoned more than whites for drug crimes at a rate of 15-1 but that, by 2016, the difference was 5-1.

Over the years that were studied, the number of black men in state prisons fell by more than 48,000 while the number of white men increased by more than 59,000. While those numbers demonstrate there is still room for significant improvement, they still don't take crime rates into account.

Wikipedia used FBI figures for its page on "Race and crime in the United States." [26] Those figures breakout as follows:

Homicide vs. Victims of Homicide by Race

Type	Black	White	Other
Homicide	52.4%	43.1%	4.4%
2007-16 Victims of Homicide	57%	40.6%	N/A

---

25 https://www.washingtonpost.com/crime-law/2019/12/04/states-imprison-black-people-five-times-rate-whites-sign-narrowing-yet-still-wide-gap/
26 https://en.m.wikipedia.org/wiki/Race_and_crime_in_the_United_States?fbclid=IwAR0ncyCPi-sN4FUWnLRIEYDQVkDfQIoZRKKgzYyH7CTb4MSk-kqtwmwYi5SA#Homicide

Fifty-two percent of violent crimes committed by juveniles are committed by blacks. Of gang members in the country, 35 percent are black, 11.5 percent are white, and 46 percent are Hispanic.

The article states that, in cases of robbery, it is 12 times more likely that the assailant is black and the victim white than vice versa. The real significance, however, is that a black person is five times more likely to commit murder or nonnegligent manslaughter.

There are a lot of numbers to digest in the previous pages. But there is another way to gauge the situation. Simply ask yourself, if you had to walk down a city street at night, and were given a choice of a low-income white, black or Hispanic neighborhood, where would you choose to go for a stroll? Even if you're black, the white neighborhood would likely win hands down.

Spike Lee made a movie in 2015 called 'Chi-Raq.' The point of the movie is obvious – poor, black neighborhoods in Chicago are virtual war zones. The same is true of poor inner-city black neighborhoods in most, if not all, major cities. These are dangerous places to live or visit.

Chapter 14
Caught in The Cycle of Violence & Poverty

Inner-city violence plays a major role in the poverty experienced in these neighborhoods. You may ask, 'Does the violence beget the poverty or does the poverty beget the violence?'

Let's suppose you want to start a business. Would you choose to setup shop in a disadvantaged neighborhood with a high violent crime rate? Certainly, you could get quite a bargain on the rent of a store, office, or manufacturing plant in such a place. You could also hire employees at a discount. Or maybe you're motivated by a desire to help the people living in that disadvantaged community. Are those motivations enough?

The reality is that you can't overlook the effects of poverty and crime. Poverty means that you're targeting a financially strapped area. Your products or services will have to fit that reality. But more than that, you can't overlook the fact that this is a high-crime neighborhood. Any savings you have on rent and wages would go to higher insurance costs, if you can find an insurance company willing to cover a business in this area at all. And then you have to worry about the safety of your employees and your customers, as well as your own safety.

Regardless of which came first, the chicken or the egg – violence or poverty – reducing violent crime is essential to changing the culture in inner-city black neighborhoods. Are white Americans to blame for the problem?

Just as the disparity of incarceration can somewhat trace its roots to the Violent Crime Control and Law Enforcement Act, inner-city violence, we can argue, can trace its roots to aspects of LBJ's 'Great Society.'

Federal assistance to poor families came with strings attached. Chief among these is the stipulation, for those receiving assistance, that requires single-parent families. The result is that it drove many black fathers out of the home. Without the influence of a father, children, particularly young black males, were set adrift without the guidance that could well have made a significant difference in the trajectories of their lives.

At the same time, while financial assistance can prove a tremendous blessing to a struggling family, at some point it shifts from a blessing to a curse. Recipients come to see the payments as an entitlement. The connection to a society that is making a concerted effort to assist them is lost, along with appreciation for the commitment of others to their welfare.

At the same time, financial assistance erodes incentive and initiative. I've told the story of how I started my business in 2008 while I was receiving unemployment benefits (you can make half again the amount of your unemployment check before you give up, dollar-for-dollar, what you make outside of unemployment benefits). Had you asked me at the time, I'd have sworn that I was working as hard as I possibly could. But, when unemployment ran out, I discovered that I could work at an entirely higher level. Necessity is a strong motivator for incentive and initiative. Initiative, as with muscles, atrophies without regular use.

Corrosive Nature of 'Entitlements'
Extends Beyond Initiative

Look at it this way; in spite of the assistance of unemployment payments when I started my company, I had a significant sense of accomplishment (even though my company hardly fits in the category of a Fortune 500 company). What sense of accomplishment is derived from cashing a welfare check from the government? If, instead of financial assistance, the government setup a business for me, provided a rent-free store filled with the products I wanted to sell, and a business plan to make it all work, what level of personal achievement could I expect other than that of not messing it up?

Handouts rob people, not only of initiative, but of the sense of pride they take in accepting a challenge. Even if they don't succeed, they have a good reason to be proud that they tried. To what degree are people in poor, inner-city black neighborhoods aware of their right to strive to achieve their dreams? To what degree have 'entitlements' blinded many to opportunities that diminish as the years go by?

While it's difficult to gauge a politician's true motives on almost any situation, beyond reasonable skepticism, it's safe to say that, in the 1960s, many politicians thought they were doing something that would work out well for disadvantaged Americans. They probably saw political opportunity in the process but still believed this was a win-win situation. Just as they thought the 1994 crime bill would work out well, they thought the 'Great Society' would benefit poor Americans, including black families.

Chapter 15
The Problem with Solving Racial Issues

Fact checkers have claimed that LBJ never said, as it is claimed, that the 'Great Society' would have "N----- voting Democrat for the next 50 years." How would the 'fact checkers' establish that he never made this statement? Were they in the room when he is alleged to have spoken? Is there any chance that political allies wouldn't come to his defense when questioned by the 'fact checkers'? If you're familiar with LBJ, this sounds precisely like something he would have said. And how have things worked out?

Until 1936, blacks largely voted Republican. An article from Salve Regina University by Daphney Daniel titled, 'How Blacks became Blue: The 1936 African American Voting Shift From the Party of Lincoln to the New Deal Coalition,' suggests that blacks switched to the Democrat Party at that time because of "Republican apathy, depression era desperation and Roosevelt's charismatic message of relief and hope." [27] In other words, the Democrats used a crisis to their advantage even back then.

Statistics, as seen in the chart below, show that, from 1936 on, the majority of blacks supported the Democrat Party (figures are difficult to find prior to that year). In other words, since 1936, Democrats have promised black Americans a better life. How then is it that, 85-years lat-

---

27 https://digitalcommons.salve.edu/pell_theses/77/?fbclid=IwAR28nUiJ_
WJsxLdX8jjJyDhyrmJYKeWevG8O4yYUO1CcyTqyk_ajA7yeYSM

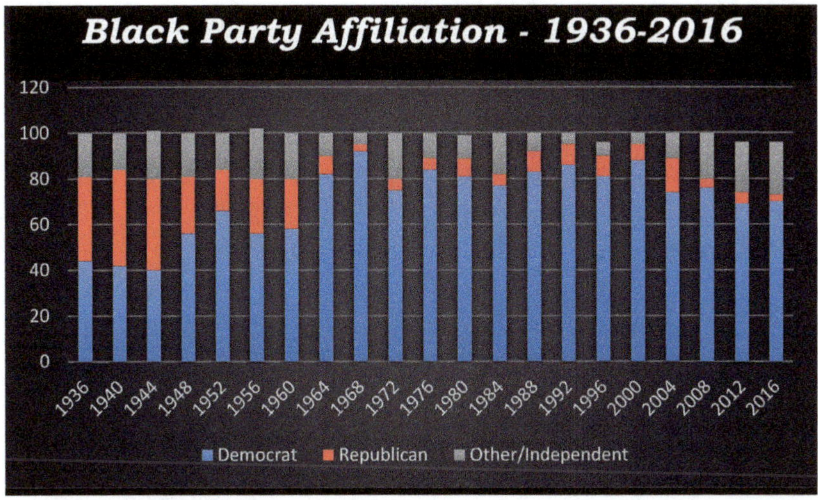

er, we're still talking about the hardships of blacks in America?

From 1933 to 1995, a 62-year stretch, there were only two times that the House was controlled by Republicans, and only eight of 34 Senates, during that stretch, saw a Republican majority. In other words, Democrats have dramatically controlled the federal legislature throughout this period. And yet Republicans are portrayed as the party where 'white guilt' most resides. [28] Considering actual Democrat control, some might suggest that the data would lead us to describe the Democrats as racial snake-oil merchants. The biggest legislative advancement of racial equality in that time, the Civil Rights Act, received proportionally more support from Republicans. And over

______

28 https://www.spokesman.com/stories/2020/jun/25/control-house-and-sen-ate-1900/

the course of American history, the Democrats have consistently served as the greatest roadblock to equal rights for blacks.

Consider a historical perspective on the connection between Democrats and racism:

- Slaveowners – predominantly Democrat
- Civil War – Confederacy dominated by Democrats while the Union was led by Republicans
- KKK – overwhelmingly dominated by Democrats
- Lynchings – dominated by Democrats
- Jim Crow Laws – instituted and enforced by Democrats
- Opposition to the Civil Rights Act – primarily from Democrats
- Support for the 1994 crime bill – primarily from Democrats

And yet, since 1933, blacks have largely, and often overwhelmingly, voted for Democrats.

At 65 (at the time of this writing), I've witnessed race as a dominant issue in America all of my life, and the issue predates my birth by at least 174 years (since the Founding of America). Blacks have voted for Democrats all of my life and longer and what have they gotten for their support? To hear them tell it, nothing. Or, at least, to hear Democrats tell us on behalf of blacks, they are in no better condition today than since the end of the Civil War or the end of Jim Crow, though the Democrats conveniently leave out the part where we acknowledge their control of the government during this period. To what degree have we moved beyond race as a problem in America? Are we looking at the question honestly? Could it be that the Democrats have used blacks to achieve power and are continuing to do so?

Have you considered what would happen to the Democrat Party if race was no longer an issue?

According to Pew Research, these were the issues that most motivated voters in the 2020 election (percentage of registered voters saying these issues are 'very important' to their vote in the 2020 presidential election) [29]:

Most Important Issues	Percentage
Economy	79
Health Care	68
Supreme Court Appointments	64
The Coronavirus Outbreak	62
Race and Ethnic Equality	59
Immigration	57
Economic Inequality	55
Climate Change	52
Abortion	52
Violent Crime	49
Foreign Policy	42
Gun Policy	40

29 https://closeup.org/wp-content/uploads/2020/08/PP_2020.08.13_voter-attitudes_4-01.png

While 'Race and Ethnic Equality' is fifth on the list above, we can argue that many of these issues are heavily weighted by consideration of racial issues. Possibly Foreign Policy and Climate Change are not. However, arguments put forth by activists and the media have suggested racial components to these issues, too. Even the Coronavirus had racial implications suggested in terms of how treatments and inoculations were administered.

Now, look back at the list of issues and imagine that race is no longer an issue. What would that do to the Democrat Party's chances in upcoming elections? Some pundits have suggested that, though the Democrats had control of the White House, Senate and House of Representatives in 2009, they didn't do anything about immigration because they didn't want to eliminate an issue that they counted on for support in upcoming elections.

If the issue of race is resolved to the relative satisfaction of all Americans, what would the loss of that issue do to the Democrat's chances at election time? Not only would blacks look at the candidates with a fresh perspective, so would many whites.

Many believe Democrats and the media distort news to create greater division along racial lines and related issues as a means of motivating voters. Without race as a factor, where would they go with their efforts to create division in America? The argument goes that Democrats remember minorities just in time for elections and forget them just as quickly after the last vote is cast.

It's also important to acknowledge that the inner cities, where blacks experience so much strife, violence and disparity, are almost universally run by Democrats. The Democrats blame America and tell Americans they need to change while the evidence suggests that Democrats are the ones who need to change the most.

Chapter 16
The Cancel Culture –
a Drag on Real Solutions?

Someone once told me, "We need to eliminate racism." What a wonderful sentiment. But, as I asked them, "How are we to do that?" You could hear the wheels grinding to a halt in their head. They hadn't really thought it out that far.

Others, no doubt, would have a series of answers – so-called solutions worked up over time. The Cancel Culture, I believe, is an outgrowth of these 'solutions.' And the Cancel Culture is a product of 'Political Correctness.' The difference between Cancel Culture and Political Correctness is that we can describe the latter more on a passive basis, and the former on a more active basis – proponents of the Cancel Culture actively seek to shut down the voices of those who dare to disagree. The goal of the Cancel Culture is to ensure that evidence contrary to the Left's agenda is not considered in public discourse.

I suspect that, when the Left introduced Political Correctness, they realized that America was not ready for the Cancel Culture. Americans were too aware of the importance of free speech and individual rights to allow that to fly. The Left identified this rugged individualism as an obstacle both to the implementation of a Cancel Culture and the ultimate goal of a pliant populace willing to accept the elitist leadership intrinsic to a socialist society.

The Leftist approach has historically run into a significant obstacle – logic. Socialism doesn't work as attempt after attempt has proven around the world. The Left will try to throw out examples to claim the opposite but, under scrutiny, their evidence doesn't pass the smell test (a fuller exploration of socialism is a topic for another book). Suffice it to say that the Left is using racism as a tool to drive America further and further into socialism. The idea that 'the American system' is to blame for racism assumes that the government should have done more about the problem. But that assumes that the government would have the power to 'fix the problem.' The Left is trying to give the government that level of power now. The assumption is that, with that power, the government can create the Leftist vision of Utopia on earth – just give the government enough power so that the world, and the people in it, are putty in the Left's hands. Therefore, the idea is that, somehow, is 'the government' can be trusted with that level of power, not just now but into the future – a somewhat precarious concept. The reality is that individual liberty is diminished in favor of a nebulous notion called 'The Greater Good.'

Considered logically, if the government can fix everything, the question follows, "Why hasn't it done so already?" The Left has provided the answer – because America is "systemically racist." These are the same people who point to the constitution as an inherently flawed document written by a bunch of old white slaveowners who wore wigs.

Some have gone as far as to suggest that America was specifically created to promote slavery and keep blacks down (The 1619 Project and CRT). If that were true, why didn't all the original colonies allow slavery when the country was founded? Why was there a long-standing fight against slavery? Why did so many Americans die in a war that decided against slavery? Why was the struggle against Jim Crow and Segregation eventually successful?

The answer, I believe, is that there's no honest way to see America and its constitution in this light. It's a stretch beyond the creditability of the wildest imagination. Rather, I believe that the constitution was divinely inspired. At a moment when those men were creating a nation, they chose to limit the power in their own hands as elected representatives of the people of that nation, as well as for future generations of elected officials. That shows a measure of wisdom and foresight at a level where historical parallels are difficult, if not impossible, to find.

They saw ultimate power as residing in 'the people.' And people, as we all know, are not perfect. Some are more flawed than others. The premise is that, when people have freedom, they will, ultimately, use it wisely. It does not mean the majority will always make good choices – the American system provides processes designed to protect the individual and a minority, though it doesn't always work out that way, at least not initially. In regard to racial relations, if the constitution were created to enforce racism, it's failed miserably.

The basis of liberty is that people get to think for themselves. Sometimes, we might not like the conclusions they draw but that's the risk of liberty. If you ensure that everyone thinks 'the right way,' you don't have liberty. In a very real sense, it doesn't matter what people think; the government will tell them what to think.

Beyond out-and-out force, there are several other tools to use when you want to effect a change in the way people think. The media, the entertainment industry, Big Tech social networks and the educational system are active in 'training people' to think 'the right way.' The latter of these is best suited to have the greatest influence over the most easily influenced audience – young Americans.

With political correctness, the message is that racism is bad. Few could reasonably argue with that sentiment. In fact, it is not a concept developed by the Left but rather one that the Left has borrowed for political advantage. They have married that idea to the 'Everyone-gets-a-trophy' philosophy that is, at its core, the basis for socialism/communism. The idea that everyone should receive the same trophy promotes the idea of equity of outcome rather than equality and opportunity. With that as a foundation of how to approach racial relations, young people have an expectation of 'social justice' and a lack of tolerance for anyone who doesn't fit in with that concept. With the Left's approach, anyone who fits their ever-broadening definition of racist is obviously evil and deserving of condemnation. And if they can't 'cancel' that person outright, at least they can 'cancel' that person's voice and ideas. What results can we expect with such an approach?

If someone does have racist ideas, can we force them to abandon their racist ideas? Or, if we have the power to try, will we merely force them to keep their racist feelings to themselves? In other words, can we achieve racial harmony by force? Can you legislate away racial animosity? How much power will we give the government in a futile effort to achieve this impossible goal?

If you look at America honestly, it's impossible not to see that racial relations have improved dramatically over the course of our history. It's not just that we elected a black president or how many blacks we have, and have had, serving in Congress, or in other offices, as well as Hispanics, Asians and other ethnic/racial groups. Only 30 or 40 years ago, an interracial relationship was liable to provoke a negative reaction from members of the community on both sides of the racial equation. Today, such relationships are commonplace. An interracial couple walks down the street and hardly anyone seems to notice or care.

This is not to suggest that there is no room for further improvement; rather, it is important that we consider the condition of racial relations in America honestly. I don't believe the Left appreciates that idea. Or maybe it's better to say that they don't want to. Just as they choose to ignore the positive aspects of America's history, in terms of race, they prefer to portray America today as a "systemically racist" nation while the Left refuses to take an honest inventory of racial relations in the country. Why would they choose to see America in the darkest racial light possible?

The answer is simple; if you wish to employ drastic measures, you first must establish the need. The Left wants America to become a socialist nation. I would say that they want America to become part of a post-national system where socialism is the global system.

Chapter 17
Never Let a Crisis to go to Waste

In 2009, speaking of the recession at the time, Pres. Barack Obama's Chief of Staff, Rahm Emanuel, said, "Never let a crisis go to waste." In reference to the COVID-19 pandemic, he repeated that statement. But if you see crisis as opportunities, why just wait for the next crisis to come along? Why not create a crisis, or multiple crisis, that you can use to achieve your political agenda? That, I believe, is the foundation of the 'America-is-systemically-racist' push today. And the proponents include the Left's army of journalists, actors/actresses and 'educators' – people who feel they could and should use their positions to influence others to agree with them, never mind that journalists abandon journalistic ethics pushing a concept rather than 'journaling' about what is happening and allowing individuals to draw their own conclusions, or 'educators' using their positions to go beyond educating students about how to think they indoctrinate them on what to think. Even actors and actresses go beyond the purview of their trade, in my opinion, when they assume to act in performances that are designed to convince people of what to think rather than to contemplate issues honestly. Additionally, they no longer seem to take entertaining the public as a serious concern; doing so is subjugated to the promotion of Leftism.

While disagreeing with the Left's negative view of the racial condition in America, once again, I'm not trying to suggest that the country has reached a point of racial nirvana. It just means that a calm and reasoned perspective is essential to ensure that we don't prescribe solutions that are actually killing the patient.

Think about taking an inventory if you owned and/or managed a store. If you fudge the numbers to fit a desired conclusion, you don't have an honest inventory and you're making decisions based on skewed figures. What kind of outcome can you expect?

Taking an honest inventory doesn't mean you can't make changes in how you run your business, or what products or services you offer to your customers. You can. But, if you don't do an honest inventory, why bother with an inventory at all. Even changes that you desire, and implement are based on an inaccurate understanding of the situation. No matter how you approach it, with a distorted inventory, it's anyone's guess what you'll wind up with.

In this light, the Left may convince us to implement all kinds of programs, and all kinds of spending, based on the idea that it will improve racial relations. But will they?

Some point to the aforementioned Civil Rights Act and LBJ's 'Great Society' as examples of measures that improved racial relations in America, but did they? Undoubtedly, they improved relations in some ways but, by their full measure, were they the right ideas? The welfare connected to LBJ's 'Great Society' is largely attributed with the disruption of two-parent families in the black community. And that is blamed as a significant factor in why, economically, blacks lag behind other racial and ethnic groups in our country. Consider the following ratios placed side by side – the ratio of unwed mothers and median annual income by race [30] [31]:

Race/Ethnicity	Unwed Mothers	Median Income
Black	69.4%	$45,438
Hispanic	51.8%	$56,113
White	28.2%	$76,057
Asian	11.7%	$98,174

As an article in MerriPedia puts it, "Single motherhood is the strongest determinant of female poverty in the United States." [32] While some have argued that this is not the cause of black poverty, it seems a bit of a stretch to downplay the effects of unwed motherhood on the economic opportunities for blacks. It goes without saying that education is often interrupted for unwed mothers.

Consider the effects of education on someone's earning potential [33]:

---

30 https://www.nationalreview.com/corner/percentage-of-births-to-unmarried-women/
31 https://www.statista.com/statistics/233324/median-household-income-in-the-united-states-by-race-or-ethnic-group/
32 http://marripedia.org/effects.of.single.parents.on.financial.stability
33 https://www.statista.com/statistics/233301/median-household-income-in-the-united-states-by-education/

Level of Education Attained	Annual Median Household Income
9th-12th Grade, No Diploma	$30,326
High School or Equivalency	$48,708
Some College	$61,911
Associates Degree	$69,573
Bachelors Degree	$100,164
Masters Degree	$117,439
Doctorate Degree	$142,347

Undoubtedly, the information above, including the percent of unwed mothers by race and median income, does not provide a complete inventory of the causal factors behind the conditions faced by blacks in America. But how can you reasonably ignore them? Only a fool, or someone devoted to seeing things otherwise, would fail to recognize the value of this information pertaining to racial relations in America. It's equally clear that this data is diminished or ignored by those pushing racial division in America.

The problem with basing change on false premises is that, eventually, and inevitably, reality will rise to the surface. When it does, people will realize they were sold a bill of goods and their reaction may prove swift and harsh. You can force someone to say they oppose racism. But a true conversion never comes from social pressure anymore than it does at the point of a gun. When people get to know each other, and see that they're generally alike in spite of any differences, they have a chance to gain greater respect for each other, even if this is not guaranteed.

The truth is that it takes time. The good news is that

Americans have made great strides in terms of racial relations, even though the Left doesn't want to acknowledge as much. The advances in improved racial relations are the foundation we should build on.

This isn't to say there is nothing to change or do at this time – that we should merely continue on our current course. To the contrary, I believe there are significant steps we can take, though they won't be easy to implement. We simply need to take care that the decisions we make are based on an honest understanding of the situation and with the absence of politics as a driving factor.

One of the most important steps we should take is to stop splitting black and underprivileged families apart. Or course, this brings up an issue that extends beyond race – welfare. We need to find a way to provide assistance to those in actual need while eliminating the requirements attached to financial assistance that separate families. In fact, the system should support the idea of keeping the family together wherever possible.

Efforts in underprivileged communities, regardless of the prominent race there, should focus on inspiring members of the community to believe that they too can succeed: encourage people to identify their dreams and then pursue them. When someone identifies a goal, the next step is to consider what they need to achieve their goal. Often, this involves a certain amount of training. Rather than pushing education that promotes social theories that inhibit personal growth, training should be specific to the individual's goals. If their dream is of a good job, with a good income, what will they require? Let's use an electrician as an example.

Electricians make a very reasonable wage. But the skills required are significant to do the job correctly, expeditiously and safely. Proper training is essential and won't happen overnight. The training will require dedication and focus. It will require accepting the responsibility of showing up and engaging their mind so that the training sticks. Remember that reaching such a goal will provide the corollary value of accomplishment, a reward in its own right. But becoming an electrician or working in construction is hardly the only direction or limit of what someone in an underprivileged community might wish to pursue. The field is wide open.

If someone has an entrepreneurial spirit, that also requires experience, dedication and careful consideration. There is no reason why anyone with a reasonable intellect couldn't achieve this goal and become their own boss. There is literally nothing they can't do if they are willing to do the groundwork required. Nothing is guaranteed but, the more they are told they can't succeed, the more likely they are to believe it. If they receive the opposite message, the more it's reinforced, the more likely they are to believe they can succeed. The surest way to fail is to fail to try.

Chapter 18
Police Abuse?

When Michael Brown was shot and killed by a police officer Aug. 10, 2014, weeks of riots erupted in cities around the country. The tragedy simultaneously launched BLM into the limelight. But as more and more information came out, it was increasingly clear that the initial reports of what happened were dramatically wide of the truth. No one, black, white, purple or green, could expect to do what Michael Brown did without seriously risking that a police officer might shoot them.

When George Floyd died in the custody of police officers May 25, 2020, riots broke out again and lasted all through the summer and warmer months of the year.

In both cases, the media seemed determined to stoke racial animosity while supporting one side of the political equation and attacking the other. Reports have since surfaced that Floyd had taken a fatal level of fentanyl. In other words, he was almost as certain to die that night if he never had an interaction with the police at all. He also had a 'heavy heart' and as much as 75-percent blockage in one artery. All this means that he was not in ideal condition for a tussle with police. But let's get back to the fentanyl.

Fentanyl is a potent opioid. It is highly addictive. It is likely to cause behavioral changes, including mood swings and other risky and dangerous behavior. To put it simply, it has the potential to hamper rational thought.

It can make it difficult for someone to concentrate or remember things. [34]

Swiftriver.com, which provided the description of the effects of fentanyl above, listed the following as "... psychological signs of fentanyl abuse":

- Confusion
- Impaired judgment
- Disorientation
- Anxiety
- Depression
- Paranoia
- Rapid mood swings
- Hallucinations

The site also lists signs of someone under the influence of fentanyl. These include labored or shallow breathing, constipation, fainting, loss of appetite, pale skin, sunken eyes, swelling of the legs, hands and feet.

While some of these signs were probably apparent to the police officers on the scene at the time of Floyd's death, it's unlikely that the police would have fully recognized that he was in the throes of a fentanyl overdose. No doubt, the optics of a smiling police officer kneeling on Floyd's neck shortly before the man died did much to incite the anger the led to night-after-night of protests and riots. But that seems to be the issue – deciphering impressions vs. reality.

Last spring, I sat down with two black men to discuss

34 https://www.swiftriver.com/fentanyl/

racial relations in light of George Floyd's death. Our discussion was amicable, but we still ran headlong into the question of impressions vs. reality. I pointed out that FBI crime statistics do not support the notion of 'systemic racism' among America's police officers. But the black men argued that the FBI was 'obviously' missing many of the instances of race-based excessive force displayed by the police. My counter to that, considering our current political environment with the media circling shark-like looking for any opportunity to pounce on a story of race-based police indiscretion, is that such stories are unlikely to go unnoticed.

I'm inclined to believe the FBI data. And what does that data show?

Total 2019 arrests and percentage of arrests (Total Above/Percent Below)

	Total	White	Black	American Indian	Asian	Native Hawaiin or other Pacific
Murder and nonnegligent manslaughter	7,964	3,650	4,078	125	83	28
	100%	45.8%	51.2%	1.6%	1.0%	0.3%
Rape	16,599	11,588	4,427	249	276	59
	100%	69.8%	26.7%	1.5%	1.7%	0.4%
Robbery	56,305	25,143	29.677	635	568	282
	100%	44.7%	52.7%	1.1%	1.0%	0.5%
Aggravated Assault	274,376	169,467	91,164	7,192	4,902	1,651
	100%	61.8%	33.2%	2.6%	1.8%	0.6%
Burglary	118,843	81,104	34,188	1,728	1,464	359
	100%	68.2%	28.8%	1.5%	1.2%	0.3%
Larceny-Theft	592,679	393,226	178,937	11,718	7,133	1,665
	100%	66.3%	30.2%	2.0%	1.2%	0.3%
Motor-Vehicle Theft	57,278	38,719	16,409	1,213	721	216
	100%	67.6%	28.6%	2.1%	1.3%	0.4%
Arson	6,291	4,453	1,553	121	125	39
	100%	70.8%	24.7%	1.9%	2.0%	0.6%
Violent Crime	355,244	209,848	129,346	8,201	5,829	2,020
	100%	59.1%	36.4%	2.3%	1.6%	0.6%
Property Crime	775,091	517,502	231,087	14,780	9,443	2,279
	100%	66.8%	29.8%	1.9%	1.2%	0.3%

(Those of Hispanic ethnicity are included within these numbers)

These numbers show that a black is about five times more likely to commit murder or 'nonnegligent manslaughter' than a white, based on the percentage of crimes committed by blacks in comparison to the percentage of blacks in America. The Left is determined to ignore this data or to flip it around to claim that white men are somehow to blame. The reality is that, when someone commits murder, they are making a choice and it is extremely rare that you would find a remotely plausible reason to blame that decision on someone else.

What would the effect on these low-income communities of color be if crime rates dropped precipitously? Would businesses show a greater interest in setting up shop in these communities if they had access to a substantial marketplace, with limited crime and an ample workforce? I suspect it would be as if the clouds parted and the sun shone through to the sound of angels playing harps and flutes with heavenly music. Let there be no mistake – such an outcome is something I greatly and dearly desire.

Mild Police Harassment?

Even in terms of the other crimes, whether whites commit more of the infractions outright, by percentage, blacks are dramatically more likely to commit these often-violent offenses. Portraying white men as somehow culpable only loosens whatever limited restraints on this behavior already exist. At the same time that Democrat controlled cities are reducing penalties for crimes, and the budget for law enforcement, they are making excuses for those who commit the crimes. They are effectively eliminating repercussions while providing a convenient excuse where someone inclined to do so can hide from a personal sense of moral responsibility.

The black men I met with last year also spoke of personal experiences with the police. They told how their sons were pulled over by the police for nothing more than driving while black. It's difficult to challenge someone's personal experience. However, reality shows that there is a subjective nature to perspectives and experiences.

I worked at a community college as the adviser to the student newspaper and taught some independent journalism classes. My boss's boss was a black man. He was, in my opinion, a great guy with a generally great attitude. But even he fell victim to the victim mentality one day.

He came to work angry one morning after receiving a ticket for driving 2 mph over the speed limit in the affluent community to the North of the college. It's a rolling, wooded area with homes valued easily in excess of $1 million each. He was certain that he received the ticket because he was black. Maybe he was right. However, as I explained to him, I knew someone who got a ticket in that village for 1 mph over the limit and they were white.

The reality is that the village in question has (or had) a reputation for giving tickets freely. Whether as a form of revenue or, more likely in my opinion, to dissuade the riff-raff from passing through the village when commuting to other parts of the county on opposite sides of the village. In terms of riffraff, I'm sure I fit the financial prerequisite for the term as well and more so than my boss's boss. In fact, the community in question is known as a home of a nationally prominent black celebrity who, no doubt, drives in the village with a feeling of impunity.

It's amazing how, if you're inclined to see something, how frequently you'll see it where, otherwise, you wouldn't notice at all. For instance, a few years back, I purchased a '93 Dodge Stealth. It's a kind of sporty car that Dodge built in collaboration with Mitsubishi; the latter built their own version, the 3000 GT, that was virtually indistinguishable unless you know what to look for. I was surprised how many Stealths and 3000 Gts I saw on the road, once I purchased a Stealth myself. Prior to that, I hardly seemed to see any at all.

An Honest Perspective on Police Shootings

Demographics of Shootings By Police				
	2017	2018	2019	2020
White	457	399	370	432
Black	223	209	235	226
Hispanic	179	148	158	156
Other	44	36	39	22
Unknown	84	204	202	163
Total	987	996	804	999

35

---

35 Statista.com (Published March 1, 2021)iot

How many of the deaths at the hands of the police, listed in the chart above, were completely justified? Some seem to suggest that anytime a black person dies at the hands of the police, it's unjustified. Of course, that's absurd. How then do we separate the justified deaths from those caused by police acting improperly?

The gauge I use is the media. It's not that I have faith in the media. Rather, it's the nature of how the media hungers for cases of the latter type. If they have any opportunity to exploit a story where a black is killed by police, the media today is all over it. Clearly, my methodology does not provide a pure picture of the situation. However, it does suggest that, when the police are wrong, it's unlikely to go unnoticed. But even that assumption appears flawed.

With George Floyd's death, even before the trial, the media had convicted former Minneapolis Police Officer Derek Chauvin. I understand that the story was largely driven by the optics involved where a police officer (Chauvin) was seen kneeling on a black man's neck. But, otherwise, there is an inconsistency to the media's apparent approach.

With the 2014 death of Michael Brown, the media was all in on the accusations of a racist reaction by the involved police officer that caused Brown's death. Even as evidence rolled out contradicting that scenario, the media wouldn't let go. They ignored news that contradicted the racist 'Narrative.' But when Walter Scott, another black man, was shot and killed by a police officer in North Charleston, SC, the evidence strongly supported the claims of a police officer abusing his authority. And yet the media did little more than cover the story. There were no riots, at least not nationally. But when Eric Garner was killed in a confrontation with police in New York, the media was all over the story. There were riots. Two NYPD officers, Officers Wenjian Liu and Raphael Ramos, were killed assassination style during the riots. But the more information came out about Garner's death, the more it was clear that no one could point to any evidence of racism as a motive of the police in the incident. Additionally, the 'chokehold' used by police in the incident was approved and the story devolved into a question of whether such chokeholds should be allowed.

The point is that the media and black activists seem to express the most outrage when the evidence does not clearly support impropriety or racism by the police. This seems to support the notion that those expressing outrage are not doing so based on an honest appraisal of any situation. It smacks of opportunism. It certainly doesn't support the notion that the police are running around in America hunting black men. That the numbers in the chart at the beginning of this section show a disparity in the numbers of shootings by race, we need only harken back to the chart from the previous section that showed a markedly higher rate of violent crime among blacks. Faced with such a reality, it is for the Left and black activists to explain away how this wouldn't influence the number of those shot by police. In fact, when compared to crime rates, the numbers of blacks killed by police is remarkably low.

The other contradiction in the media's handling of shootings by police is where whites are involved. July 26, 2021, two months after Floyd died, and during the summer-and-longer riots, 19-year-old Zachary Hammond, though unarmed, was shot and killed by an officer in South Carolina. Before reading his name here, did you ever hear of him before? How about Tony Timpa? Have you heard his name before?

The headline in the *MTO News* (Most Visited African American News Network), reads, "Police Murder White man, Tony Timpa, Same Way As George Floyd." As the story explains, "The bodycam footage shows Tony Timpa begging and pleaded for help more than 30 times as Dallas police officers pressed his neck to the ground. His nose was buried in the grass was drawing his last breaths." The story goes on to say that the charges against the four officers involved were dropped. [36]

Another story in The Mercury News has the headline, "When the victim is white and the cop is black, the response has been different." This is a story of how Minneapolis police officer Mohamed Noor, a black man, fatally shot Justine Damond, who was white. [37] The shooting

36 https://mtonews.com/police-murder-white-man-tony-timpa-the-way-they-killed-george-floyd-video
37 https://www.mercurynews.com/2017/08/02/in-minneapolis-a-different-police-shooting/

was described as totally unjustified; Damond was an innocent bystander. But were there riots or even "mostly
peaceful protests"? Not a one.

Take a Walk in Their Tactical Leather Boots

Whites are often told these days that we can't comment
on the black condition in America because we're not black
(never mind that blacks seem entitled to comment on the
white condition, and guilt, without restraint). But what
about commenting on the experience of police officers? To
what degree are we qualified to comment on their experiences without taking a walk in their hybrid moccasins
for a while?

Leftist activists and the media vociferously assail police with a constant barrage of criticisms these days. As
a result, police recruitment is down while early retire-
ments are up. I was never a police officer. However, I suspect that police are supportive of other police not simply
because they're sticking up for their own.

They know what a police officer goes through. A police
officer working in 'ChiRaq' has an extremely dangerous
job. These days, with the anti-police rhetoric, the hazards
of the profession are even greater. I don't envy them. I
wouldn't even try doing their job. But I am able to understand, somewhat, what they're going through.

Ask yourself, when was the last time someone got in
your face. I mean really, up in your face – angry, spit
flying with insults, their eyes bulging, veins throbbing at

their temples and their body language suggesting they could make the transaction from a verbal to a physical attack at any moment?

Many of us have experienced someone in this frame of mind at some point in our lives. Imagine having these kinds of aggressive interactions on a regular basis. Imagine knowing that it's not out of the realm of possibility for the raging individuals to cross that line. They may pull weapons when they do cross the line. Imagine that someone won't wait for the verbal confrontation; an officer will pull a car over or approach a home on a domestic call, and someone will start shooting when the officer is out in the open walking toward the vehicle or the residence.

As I've put it, and strictly as a matter of self-preservation, if I were a cop in the inner city, I would be the most trigger-happy SOB you ever met. It's a remarkable testament to the professionalism of our police force in this country that they display what is actually an incredible degree of restraint in the face of the violence they see on the streets day after day. I think it's a miracle the police are even half as restrained as they are.

At the same time, I'll acknowledge that there are times when police do not act with the strict professionalism we expect of them. In some cases, I suspect the pressure is too much and, in a particular circumstance, they snap. After all, they are human. And yet, there are still what I'll call bad cops – people who shouldn't be in uniform at all.

According to statista.com, there were 697,195 full-time

law enforcement officers in the U.S. in 2019. To expect that we wouldn't find some bad apples in a bunch that size is not reasonable. If only one percent of them were unfit for duty in law enforcement, that would represent approximately 7,000 bad police officers. But it would leave more than 690,000 qualified professionals helping to keep our streets safe.

Personally, I'm angered anytime I hear of police behaving badly. When I hear of police taking kickbacks or bribes, I hope that they're held accountable. When I hear of physical abuse by police, I want justice to be served, regardless of the color or ethnicity of those involved. But I have learned to approach these events with caution. I will not paint police officers with the brush of guilt until I've heard more about what transpired.

Was the officer pushed over the edge to the point where they 'snapped'? Even if they did, this isn't much of an excuse in my book because professionalism requires that they don't 'snap.' Whatever the situation, it's not okay, though somewhat humanly understandable in some cases, for a police officer to lose control. When they 'snap,' they abandon professionalism. However, if they react in self-defense, or to defend a partner or the public, that strikes me as a reasonable use of force. The problem is that such cases are not always clear cut. And it's unfair, as members of the general public, for us to expect them always to err on the right side of the issue when they are forced to make spur-of-the-moment decisions when lives and safety hang in the balance.

I do not make excuses when a police officer does act improperly. Professionalism does not make room for racial discrimination. But I do believe all police officers are entitled to a fair trial. In today's environment, when the situation involves a black man, a fair trial is increasingly unlikely for the police officer(s) involved. The media consistently convicts them in public without a trial and often with errant references to evidence.

As the data we've already discussed here indicated, at the very least, accusations of widespread racially motivated police violence are greatly exaggerated. Is there room for improvement? Of course. But the solution isn't to 'Defund the Police.' A solid police presence in inner cities is more vital to the public safety today than ever. If we're ever going to break the cycle of poverty and violence in inner-city neighborhoods, the police will play an integral role in that process. I would say that the police need the support of the communities where they serve in order to remind them of the need to live up to the highest standards of professionalism. Attacks on the police based on false information have the opposite effect and are dramatically counterproductive.

Chapter 19
The Hypocrisy of WOKEness

When you see BLM members protesting, or rioting, as the protests always seem to devolve into, you see many whites in among the crowds. In white neighborhoods where they have held BLM protests, the marchers are almost exclusively white. In 2020, it's said that $90 million was donated to BLM. Let's skip over the part where founders of the group admit that they are communists and that China's CCP has financially backed the group, does marching in a BLM protest or donating to BLM absolve a white person of their 'white guilt?' Is that all it takes?

The current Cancel Culture seems to imply that, if you're white, you're guilty of racism and nothing you can do will completely remove the stain of racism from your soul. For starters, everything in your life was built on the backs of blacks.

The 'WOKE' community appears to accept this premise without question (in fact, it's the nature of the Cancel Culture not to question anything). Let's suppose, as whites, we accept this idea. What should we do about it?

If white people truly feel this way, is it enough to 'acknowledge their guilt?' Does acknowledgment, marching in a protest and sending in a few dollars cover the costs associated with that guilt?

Maybe it's a question of garnering sufficient 'Virtue

Points' to clear your conscience and set things right with blacks in our society? Maybe we should establish the required number of 'Virtue Points' to achieve racial forgiveness? Then we can create a point system determining how many points you'll receive for particular acts. For instance ...

Virtue Signaling Point Chart

Virtue Signaling Act	Value
Comment on your sense of racial remorse	1
Contribute to BLM (per $100)	1
Contribute to NAACP (per $100)	1
Let a black person get in front of you in line	1
Call out Trump or Trump supporter as racist	2
Tell someone that America is systemically racist	2
March in a BLM protest	2
Join in BLM riot	4
Total Required for Racial Absolution	120

This chart may require some adjustment as, currently, someone could buy their way free of white guilt with a mere $12,000. That seems a bit low. And with four points per BLM riot participation, is it safe to assume we'll see more such riots, and with far-higher levels of participation?

Of course, the idea of assigning specific points to acts of racial Virtue Signaling is ridiculous. And could we really find a number that would suffice to render someone's soul free of racial guilt, if we accept the basis for that guilt? In reality, if we accept the notion of 'white guilt,' would 'Virtue Signaling' work as a form of penance at all? Isn't it inherently deficient?

If someone believes in 'white guilt,' don't they need to undo the damage to the best of their ability?

Let's suppose we're talking about someone who stole a family heirloom from your grandmother when she was young. Instead of your grandmother handing the valued item to you, the thief handed the heirloom down to their descendants. If you discovered that they had your family heirloom, would it be enough if they merely said, "I'm sorry" and then kept the item in their family? Wouldn't you expect them to give the item back to its rightful owners?

In other words, for those who buy into 'white guilt,' they own the hypocrisy of 'White Guilt' and WOKEness. They claim to have identified a wrong but, rather than doing everything in their own power, or even anything of substance, to absolve themselves of the guilt they've identified, they look to the government to spread the cost of compensation around to everyone, even those who don't accept their premise of guilt. Is such a person deserving of racial absolution or respect? Not from my perspective.

I would have far more respect for them if they set about righting the wrong with respect to their own level of guilt. In other words, give up that 5,000-square-foot home on three exclusive acres to an underprivileged family. Then move into that family's inner-city apartment. Leave your

Q7 Audi or RX Hybrid Lexus to them and drive off in their '97 Toyota Camry with the mismatched right fender and door.

I would respect that. I would find doing so the epitome of foolishness, but at least I wouldn't see them as blatant hypocrites.

Making a commitment to improve racial relations is a worthy cause, though I'll personally continue to judge people according to their individual merits of character and in as colorblind a fashion as possible. And, if it's all the same to you, and even if it isn't, I'll approach the issue without the least sense of guilt.

Chapter 20
And Then Came CRT

I bring up the topic of CRT – Critical Race Theory – late in this piece because it wasn't a term I was familiar with when I first wrote the draft of a Neanderthal's thoughts on race. Its placement late in the book should not imply a lower priority for this topic.

To discuss CRT, we must first identify the term. My understanding is that the basis of CRT is a theory that America was founded based not on principles of liberty but to defend and promote racism. CRT goes as far as to suggest that, rather than fighting for liberty, the Founding Fathers went to war against England over a threat that Parliament would legislate away the 'rights' of colonists to own slaves.

The preceding pages should represent a sufficient response to this absurd notion. The mere fact that we, as a nation, have considered the concept of improved racial relations as reasonable of our time and effort flies directly in the face of the premise that America was founded based on racism. The inclusion of the 3/5ths Compromise does not support the idea of a racist country, it flies in the face of such a theory. It stands as an example of the need for a compromise due to a disparity of perspectives on the issue of slavery. If no one objected to slavery, why would we need a compromise at all?

As with WOKEness and Cancel Culture, CRT comes

with the convenient caveat that the only people who would dare to challenge the theory are those who are obviously racists. It's set up to intimidate and silence those with opposing views. Once again, as pointed out earlier, this demonstrates a lack of confidence in the argument. If they truly believed in CRT they would want those who don't buy the theory to exhaust themselves battering their heads against the immutable truths of CRT. There are no such truths so they do all they can to avoid the challenges that are sure to expose it for what it is – a lie and a fabrication.

Starting with the school board in Loudon, VA, parents have accused their school districts of pushing CRT on their children. The school boards have generally denied these charges. But, what has generally proven the case, even if the school district isn't using the term 'Critical Race Theory' in their lessons, they are still pushing the concepts of CRT. In several cases, this has been proven when groups have gotten their hands on the material used by teachers that explicitly include reference to teaching CRT. But we don't really need to see that material to know that the school boards are uniformly lying; the evidence is all around us.

The evidence is on the street. If you speak with teens who are in high school, or even junior high, or those who have recently graduated, you will find that they are widely sold on the idea of CRT. They may have heard of the term outside of the school's walls but they wouldn't be such devout disciples of CRT if it wasn't at the core of what they're learning in our schools.

CRT can also be described, and has been described, as the premise that we can fight racism with racism. White children are taught that, based on CRT, they are privileged oppressors. Black and brown children are taught that they are victims of oppression. Resentments and guilt are reinforced. And, behind it all, the cure is socialism/Marxism.

Along with their zombie-like faith in CRT, those I've spoken with have also shown a distinct reluctance to discuss the issue. They are offended that I would challenge their racial religion and often cast me as an obvious racist in their eyes for daring to question the theory. They often categorize me as an old racist who is inflexible in my perspectives when it is actually a case of their own inflexibility. I have said this to them, as I pose to the reader now, if you can convince me that I'm wrong, I will change my course abruptly.

In reality, CRT is just another way of packaging racial grievances. I would say that the race baters have reached a new low. Another way to put it is that CRT is putting Howard Zinn's *A People's History of the United States* on steroids. Zinn, described by some as a socialist, and by others as a communist, wrote his textbook through the prism of racism, as though every aspect of America's history must be viewed through the lens of racism if we are to see it's truth. Zinn's textbook has been widely used by school districts throughout the country for years. Of course, we know that Zinn was correct because Jason

Bourne said so when talking to his psychiatrist in *'Good Will Hunting.'* But, if you'll pardon my snarkiness, this is what the Left has done with the book. From the movie to Leftist educators, his textbook has been presented as a groundbreaking perspective that provides a truer understanding of American history. Hogwash. Zinn was nothing more than a political activist who rewrote history to fit his socialist agenda.

Whether we're talking about 'A People's History of the United States' or CRT, the point is that neither should expect to escape intellectual challenges. And yet they come with that expectation as though only opposing views are required to stand up on their own intellectual feet.

A Deplorable Neanderthal Summarizes

Let's say that the figures I shared in the chapters above all overstate the actual numbers of black crime, police shootings, demographics of income, lynching, et cetera; does that change the story? I haven't denied race-based disparities. I believe a person would be hard pressed to suggest I didn't try to take an honest appraisal of America's racial history and the status of race today. Good and bad – I've tried to include it all. I believe that I've lived up to the notion of taking an honest inventory. But even if the figures used in the preceding pages are off, it's clear that America is not 'systemically racist.'

A 'systemically racist' nation does not argue and debate over slavery until it erupts into a war that takes the lives of a significant portion of its population. It does not pass laws to give 'the other race' equal rights. It does not have a significant portion of its population opposing Jim Crow and Segregation. And it doesn't spend one minute allowing people to call its majority population racially guilty.

The reality is that there wouldn't be any racial tension in America if our Founders hadn't created a country based on the concept of liberty. It is only through the prism of liberty that equal rights for a group, or an individual, matter. It is only based on the concept of liberty that America is held accountable for its past or current racial conditions. Without the principle of liberty, none of this matters. Without liberty, racial equity is left to the whim of the oligarchs, monarchs and dictators.

It is fair to hold America accountable for failing to fully live up to the standards she set for herself but then it was never a question that America might perfectly apply liberty. The Founders knew this, which is why they limited the power of the government.

The founders of BLM acknowledge that they are trained as Marxist activists and are seeking to transform America into a Marxist nation. The people who support BLM, whether they realize it or not, are supporting the core principle of Marxism where equity of outcome, regardless of effort, skill or initiative applied, is the guiding standard. The point that they miss, ignore or eagerly embrace, is that, under the system they promote, there is no way for people experiencing such restrictions on their liberty to have redress. Inequities are baked into the cake and will only change based on the fancy of the Marxist 'leadership.' After all, even in a Marxist system, the government is comprised of people with all the flaws and frailties of people in any other system.

Rather than a history of 'systemic racism,' America has a history where the principle of liberty has survived, certainly tarnished at times, for going on two-and-a-half centuries. It's a remarkable accomplishment. The only problem is that there are many in our society who refuse to see that reality.

Is there more we should do to reduce racism and promote racial equality in America? Of course. But there have always been Americans who have acknowledged as much. No, BLM, Antifa and the Left today did not invent the idea of racial equality, though they have bastard-ized it with 'everybody-gets-a-trophy' notions of equity in place of equality.

Equality is the concept that everyone has an equal right to pursue happiness. It doesn't mean that we all start from the same place. And it doesn't mean that we are guaranteed the same outcome. With a guarantee of out-come, there's no point in the journey. In reality, there's little purpose in life if everything is handed to us. Is all we require in life food, clothes, a place to live and our other necessities?

It's my theory that, in spite of all the very real trials faced by many poor inner-city blacks, there are those among them who have achieved true happiness beyond the capacity of some rich whites in affluent neighbor-hoods. This isn't to downplay the value of economic suc-cess. But it is to say that happiness isn't necessarily de-pendent on how much money someone has. As flawed individuals, we often have difficulty in recognizing what matters most.

That said, I strongly believe that there are changes re-quired in the way we, as a society, approach those strug-gling with poverty, regardless of the color or ethnicity of those who are struggling. I believe that inspiration has dramatically more value than 'entitlements.' You can put a dollar value on a handout, though even that value is largely dependent on how it is used. But a frame of mind that embraces achieving personal peace and initiative is, as they say in the Mastercard commercials, "Priceless."

Additional training for police to help them to avoid situations where split-second, life-and-death decisions are required is high on my list of suggestions for our country. But that comes with a decision to give police the support they deserve. Yes, we need to hold bad cops accountable. Professionalism in our police force does not have room for racism. But we have to consider the situation honestly, which will lead us to the quick understanding that our police are there to protect the innocent while getting the guilty and dangerous off the streets. And we need to give America the respect that she is due.

Cynicism is rampant in our society today, and much of it justified. But cynicism has a corrosive effect. Cynicism is what I call *Intellectual Surrender*. It justifies the worst behaviors. This is evident even among our elected officials. They condemn the system as broken, and this provides the wiggle room for them to see their positions opportunistically. In other words, justified or not, we need to resist cynicism. Standing against cynicism starts with the individual. If you wait around for others to join you in that fight, you'll never take the first step, and no one will ever have an example to follow.

Yes, America has fallen short of its principles to the extent that there is room for criticism (the Founders would have told you to expect that). But shouldn't that criticism be constructive? If we tear America down now, what will we replace it with? Will that new system fix the problems we've identified? But, in the process, will it also include checks and balances to ensure that it doesn't transform into a tyrannical monster we can't control or escape?

There are people in America seeking to realize that transformation. As one person I've heard of put it, "Socialism is a system you can join freely but you need a gun to escape." Whether we would ever take up arms to restore our nation to the principle of liberty or not is a matter of speculation. What is not speculation is that, if the people wanting to transform America are successful, that is the choice we will face. To avoid that possible eventuality, Americans need to stand up to the 'Cancel Culture.' In a clear and loud voice, they need to state that America is not a 'systemically racist' nation. And they need to refuse to accept the 'White Guilt' those who seek to divide us are trying to push.

Racial attitudes of the past were based on a toxic mix of arrogance and ignorance. Consider the early interactions of Westerners with other cultures and groups. The Westerner comes from a culture of manufacturing, science, institutes of education, and what we now call classical music. The differences were unmistakable when the Westerner met someone living in a hut with a mud floor who has no more concept of firearms than of how to read sheet music. The ignorance for the Westerner was that he or she couldn't see how historically close behind them was their own dirt-floored hut, spears and arrows. And that was also the arrogance.

Those who attack America today as "Systemically Racist" are suffering from an equally toxic mix of arrogance and ignorance. They utterly fail to see that it would be historically unlikely that disparate racial and ethnic groups would meet and mix without any conflicts. Through their ignorance, and their arrogance, they fail to see that there's no reason to think they'd have done any better if they were in the shoes of our American Forefathers. Their condemnation is based on a one-sided and unrealistic approach to history. And this arrogance and ignorance ensures that we are basing our decisions on lies and half truths. It is optimistic beyond all reason to think that anything good would come of that. In the meantime, we are also diverted from seeking solutions that are based on honest appraisals.

The comparison is of two shop owners. Both conduct a monthly inventory - an appraisal of how their business has done for the last month. An honest appraisal will allow them to order new products that are more likely to sell. But, for the store owner who allows wishful thinking to dominate their process of taking inventory, that disingenuous process will cause them to order products that are unlikely to sell. If they don't rectify the problem soon enough, their business will fail.

We need an honest inventory of American history to make decisions that will benefit our country and its people. Even other countries will benefit from observing how we honestly conduct ourselves. But, if we continue to rely on a dishonest inventory, we set ourselves on a path that takes us down a road to ruin where the only equality we see is the equity of misery. If we don't take an honest inventory, we set ourselves up for cultural bankruptcy.

And the longer it takes to get there, the more we will suffer along the way and will have to struggle to get back on the right road afterwards.

NOTE: This is the first in a series of 'Deplorable Neanderthal Contemplates ..." books where the author, Richard Rostron, will seek to conduct an honest inventory of problems confronting our culture, society and nation.

About the Author

Richard Rostron's two-decade career as a journalist includes five years as a freelancer on contract with *The Chicago Tribune*. He was also sports editor with a small independent weekly newspaper for five years and is currently the managing editor/publisher of *The Response*, a mostly Online publication that 'responds' to the bias in the media. He also served as a freelance writer with numerous other publications, including *The Daily Herald* (third behind the *Tribune* as Illinois' largest daily newspaper), *Easyriders* and other magazines. Of these, he is active yet with *The Response* with which he hopes to offset some of the damage done by the media's partisan approach to the truth and the news.

He previously ghost wrote books about choosing a senior home and starting an ATM business. He ghost wrote a biker novel titled *Banshee Riders* under the pseudonym Peter Albert Derringer. Most recently, he completed a novel for teens titled *The Burning Sea of Iron Bottom*

Bay, a novel of historical fiction about a great-grand-father sharing his experiences in the US Navy during WWII with his great-grandson and the great-grandson's best friend. While planning additional *Deplorable Neanderthal Contemplates ...* books, his true passion is writing books of historical fiction for teens, whom he feels are not hearing these stories of courage and dedication to liberty and individual freedoms. He recently completed a research trip to New England for several books he plans to write for teens about the American Revolution and the Civil War.

Along with publishing *The Response,* and writing the *Deplorable Neanderthal Contemplates ...* series of books, he feels that writing books that honestly examine American history, even if on a fictional basis, is something that is desperately needed today. He challenges readers to wander in among the shelves of their local library to see what is available for young readers. Rostron did so and narrowly avoided the shock of doing so because he anticipated that WOKEness and the Left's heavy influence would have preceded him. Books about LGBTQ and racial relations in America, particularly those that portray America in a wholly negative light, overwhelmingly dominated what he saw there.

Rostron welcomes feedback on this and other writings. You can send your comments to:
burningseaofironbottombay@gmail.com.

Other Books From Padowski Publications

Naval history explodes from the pages of *The Burning Sea of Iron Bottom Bay* as a great-grandfather shares his experiences in the US Navy during WWII with his great-grandson and a friend. But, in the process, the boys get more than a history lesson; they also learn about dealing with challenges today.

By Rich Rostron

Get your copy today on Amazon.

A young man begins to grow up in one of the most unlikely of places - in an outlaw motorcycle club.

By Peter Albert Derringer

Also available on Amazon.